UNDERSTANDING THE TRINITY

Understanding the Trinity

ALISTER MCGRATH

KINGSWAY PUBLICATIONS
EASTBOURNE

ISBN 0 86065 512 1

Produced by Bookprint Creative Services
P. O. Box 827, BN21 3YJ, England, for
KINGSWAY PUBLICATIONS LTD
Lottbridge Drove, Eastbourne, E. Sussex BN23 6NT.
Printed in Great Britain.

For

Elizabeth

Contents

Preface

'If you can understand it, it's not God!' (Augustine of Hippo). Augustine rightly pointed out that no human mind could ever fully comprehend God, but we must at least *try* to understand who God is and what he is like. The Christian understanding of God, culminating in the doctrine of the Trinity, is remarkably deep and rich, and the reader must be warned from the beginning that the best that this book can do is to scratch the surface. But it is written in the belief that it may be helpful to those who find difficulty in thinking about God, and especially the doctrine of the Trinity. I hope that it will cast at least a little light on these areas, and perhaps even stimulate the reader to think more about them. The reader who found my earlier book *Understanding Jesus* helpful may well find that the present book will further help him both in understanding his own faith and explaining it to others. If it manages to do either of these, it will have served its purpose well.

All too often, books dealing with the doctrine of the Trinity assume that their readers already know *why* they believe in the doctrine, so that all that needs to be done is to explain the doctrine. The present book is written in the belief that the best way of understanding what the doctrine of the Trinity is all about is to wrestle with why Christians believe in this doctrine in the first place. The book begins by considering how it is that we know, speak and think about God in the first place —and shows how the idea of God as a Trinity is presupposed even at this stage. As the book progresses, it will become increasingly clear that the doctrine of the Trinity is simply the believer's final word about the God whom he knows, loves and adores.

ALISTER MCGRATH

I

God and His Critics

Every newspaper dreads publishing an obituary before its subject has actually died! The story is told of a famous London newspaper which published the obituary of a noted politician. Later that morning, the editor received an outraged phone call from the man himself. 'I've just read my own obituary in your paper,' he told the unfortunate editor. 'I see,' came the reply. 'And may I ask where you are speaking from?' And we all know of Mark Twain's famous cable from Europe to the Associated Press: 'The report of my death was an exaggeration.'

In the 1960s a whole host of articles and books appeared, announcing that 'God was dead'. Looking back on those days, it rather looks as if this death was an event engineered by the media. The power of the media—both press and television—to change, rather than just report, what happens is legendary. For instance, a well-known newspaper editor is once alleged to have told his staff to get busy covering the war in Cuba. 'But there isn't a war in Cuba!' his astonished staff replied. 'Well,' he riposted, 'we can soon change that.' Publicizing John Robinson's book *Honest to God* (S.C.M. 1963), the *Sunday Observer* declared, 'our image of God must go'. Robinson's book was little more than a confused sketch of what he thought some modern theologians were saying—but by the time the *Observer* had finished with it, the very existence of Christianity seemed overnight to depend upon it. A similar situation developed in the United States. *Time Magazine*, soon to be followed by *The New Yorker* and the *New York Times*, looking for a suitable headline to a report in its religion section on the ideas of a few angry young theologians, reached for the nearest cliché and declared the existence of the 'death of God' school. The curious American public were treated to intense, sombre discussion of the course theology would take 'after the death of God'.

These reports of the death of God, however, turned out to be a little premature. The 'death' was, in fact, something of a non-event, and the whole 'death of God' debate is now generally regarded as telling us much more about North American and European society in the 1960s than about God. 'God is dead'—the slogan so familiar to those who lived in the 1960s —really means 'I don't find God a personal reality any more', or 'the society in which I live doesn't need God any more'. But if this is the criterion which determines whether God is 'dead' or not, it is obvious from the expansion of Christianity since then that God is very much alive. The talk about 'a world come of age' which doesn't need God any more, seems strange and out of place in the sober realism of today, so different from the optimism of the 1960s. Similarly, we hear much from the 'death of God' school about the inability of 'modern man' to make sense of the word 'God'. But just who is this 'modern man'? All too often he seems to be some Oxford don pontificating over a glass of port in his senior common room about the meaninglessness of words—someone who has never experienced God at first-hand, but just reads about him at second-hand in books. It is remarkably difficult for anyone who has first-hand experience of the living God to think of him as being 'dead'.

God obstinately refuses to show any signs of *rigor mortis*. There is just no way that the church can be described as finding itself stuck with the corpse of God on its hands: indeed, the resurgence and growth of faith throughout the world-wide church points to his vitality. God is *living*—he is *alive*. God's obituary has been frequently penned since the dawn of the Enlightenment of the eighteenth century by those who believed that they had finally killed him off. But just like the boy who cried 'Wolf!' so often that everyone stopped listening to him, so we need to be more than a little sceptical about these declarations of God's demise. 'What—is God dead *again*?' we might well ask. In reply we are assured that God is *really* dead this time round—that is, until the next time. The impression given is that God is in some sort of coma, so that it's just a matter of time before he dies—but the reality is that God gives every indication of being very much alive. In fact, the indications are that the obituary of the 'death of God' school has already been written and published, while a far from dead God continues to excite and arouse a new generation of believers. 'God is dead' is dead.

What do we mean when we talk about 'God' anyway? There is a tendency on the part of many—especially those of a more philosophical inclination—to talk about God as if he was some sort of *concept*. But it is much more accurate to think of God as someone we *experience* or *encounter*. God isn't an idea we can kick about in seminar rooms—he is a living reality who enters into our experience and transforms it. Our experience of God is something which we talk about with others, and our encounter with him is something which we can try to put into words, but behind our ideas and words lies the greater reality of God himself. A visitor to the Taj Mahal may try and describe what he saw, putting it into words, however, what is important to him is not so much the words he uses but what he is trying to describe in those words. Let's develop this point a little.

Suppose you were with Napoleon Bonaparte as he began his triumphant Hundred Days in France, after escaping from exile in Elba. From all the accounts we possess of that remarkable period in modern French history, it is clear that Napoleon exercised a remarkable influence over all whom he encountered. It is probable that he would have made an equally deep impression upon you. You then try to put that experience, that encounter, into words, and—like so many biographers—find yourself constantly unable to express fully the greatness of that person. Although you try, you are always painfully aware that you are unable to describe adequately your experience of the personal reality of Napoleon. Words can neither capture nor convey your experience in a complete and satisfactory way. But let us suppose you then meet someone else who had also been with Napoleon during those eventful Hundred Days. Now, suddenly, you are able to share a common experience. No longer do you need to describe it to each other, because you both share the experience of the encounter with this individual. You can develop what you already have, swapping stories about what happened and helping each other further to understand what went on at the time. Now words can *re*capture that experience—an experience they couldn't really *capture* in the first place.

It's the same with all the great experiences of life—the experiences that really matter, that change people. You can share them with others, but it is very difficult to describe them. I remember once asking an older friend what it was like living in London during the blitz in the Second World War. After several attempts to describe what it was like, he gave up, saying, 'It's no use—unless you actually lived through it, you can't understand what it was like.' Encountering and experiencing God is exactly like this: it is something exceptionally difficult to describe, but it is something which is very easy to share with someone who has already had that experience. It is for this reason that talking about God is so difficult. Christians find it difficult to describe their experience of God to their non-Christian friends simply because there is no point of contact, no common ground, on which they can build.

Many of us have been subjected to what is probably one of the most subtle of modern tortures—having to listen to someone describe their holiday experiences, or look at somebody else's vacation photographs. It's just one of those things that you have to put up with if you don't want to spoil your friendship. And so you listen to them as they ramble on at great length about the Tower of London, or show a colour transparency of the Great Pyramid: 'Sorry it's out of focus—you can just see me behind that camel there.' There is no point of contact between you and your friends, and you find yourself becoming increasingly bored. But then the situation suddenly changes: they start talking about the Oxford colleges—and you were there as a student. As you realize that you share a common experience or encounter, that you have something in common, the situation is transformed.

Again, it's like being at a party and finding yourself trapped with someone and having to talk to them. You've never met them before, and after a few minutes you rather wish it had stayed that way. The conversation falters somewhat as you each try to think of something to talk about. Then you discover that you both know the same person well—and suddenly conversation becomes a lot easier. Each of you may see him in a different light, but it's the same person you're both talking about. What the other says ties in with what you already know about that person, and may even help you understand or know him better.

And so it is with God. When Christians talk about God, they're not discussing an idea or a concept, but an encounter, an experience, which they share. It's like talking about a friend they have in common. Even though they may perceive God in slightly different ways, there's no doubt that they're talking about the same person, the same experience, the same encounter—and what one says may help someone else gain a deeper understanding of what God is like.

Perhaps we ought to clear up a possible misunderstanding at this point. When we talk about 'experiencing God', we're not saying that our present experience—whatever that may be like—is God. What we are saying is that it is possible to experience God, not that God is to be identified with our experiences. Liberal theology has a tendency not merely to discover but also to define God in terms of present experience. Thus the nineteenth-century theologian Schleiermacher spoke of God as the origin of a 'feeling of absolute dependence', while the noted American liberal Paul Tillich referred to God as 'the experience of the unconditioned'. Recently a New York theologian suggested that his experience of an 'energy that has no name' on stepping out of his bath was an experience of God (rather than of the undoubtedly high quality of New York City water).

How can—and how dare—this theologian identify God with his experience on getting out of his bath? In saying that, he and others make the existence of God virtually dependent upon present experience and private judgement. And when such liberal theologians fail to experience such 'energy that has no name' on getting out of their bath, they start writing about the 'death of God' or the 'experience of the absence of God', when what they really ought to be writing about is the total inadequacy of liberal thinking about who God is and what he is like! For God's existence is prior to and independent of our experience of him. Psalm 42 is a deeply moving account of the Psalmist's conviction that God *is there,* even though he does not *experience him as present* here and now. Scripture affirms that God encounters us and we experience that encounter, but not that our everyday experience defines what God is like. Our experience of encountering God is not a private experience either, but one shared with others—their experience confirms and extends ours. An illustration will help bring this point out.

I remember once reading a book about the British scientific intelligence network during the Second World War. It was a rather entertaining book, and I enjoyed reading it. Even though I knew next to nothing about the scientific principles at stake, I could follow the book and learned a lot from it. At one point the author describes how he had to travel by air from one part of England to another to attend a special meeting—and I suddenly began to read the book more carefully, for I realized that I knew the pilot of the plane. After the war he had taken up a university post at Oxford, and I knew him as a delightful but slightly scatterbrained academic. The author described several of the crazy things this pilot did, and I can remember thinking, 'He's *still* just like that!' Two points stood out for me. First, the book suddenly became more interesting because it was talking about someone I knew. Secondly, what was said both confirmed and extended my knowledge of that person: it was consistent with what I already knew, and told me more about him.

In many ways this little episode illustrates how Christians think about God. As they read the Bible they encounter someone they *know*, someone who stands out from its pages as a living reality in their experience. And what they read extends and develops their knowledge of that person. It is worth noting that Christians have always talked about *knowing* God—not just *knowing about*, but *knowing*. We may know a lot about someone, and yet not know him—just as we may know someone, but not know very much about him. I can open the *Encyclopedia Britannica* and find out an enormous amount about some important historical figure, like Napoleon Bonaparte or George Washington, but that doesn't mean that I know them. Many of us have had the experience of meeting someone at a party and getting to know them as a person, yet managing to find out very little about him. And it's surprising how little husbands really know about their wives, as I keep discovering.

We can identify two main ways in which we get to know a person. First, we may be told a lot about this person, so that when we meet him we already know exactly who he is and can develop the relationship from that point. Secondly, we may meet someone about whom we know nothing or very little, and discover that we can relate to them as a person—and as that relationship develops, so we discover more about them. And so it is with God. Many people know a lot about God— they may read their Bibles or talk to individuals who have had a deep and real experience of God. But they have yet to have this experience for themselves—they have yet to *encounter* God. Then, when that encounter occurs, they know exactly what has happened and who it is that they have encountered, and can take the relationship on from that point. 'Knowing' means encountering and experiencing someone. Knowledge *about* God and knowledge *of* God are combined, as factual knowledge and encounter together make up our knowledge of and relationship with the person of God.

Alternatively, we may encounter God and yet not realize quite what has happened. When I was a child I can remember being told the story of Cinderella, who goes to Prince Charming's ball incognito. There, she and the prince fall in love. Although the prince doesn't know who she is, there is no contradiction involved: falling in love doesn't depend upon knowing everything about someone, but upon the way in which you experience that person. And that is very often what happens with God. We encounter him, perhaps very suddenly, and our relationship with him begins. As is often the case, 'faith is caught, not taught'. After this initial encounter, we then start to learn more about God.

Let's go back to our Cinderella story for a moment. After the prince had fallen in love with her, despite her midnight flight from the ball, he was determined to find out more about her—such as who she really was, for a start. He needed a name to put to the girl he'd fallen in love with. This sort of experience is recounted in both the Old and New Testaments. Someone experiences something, encounters someone and then realizes that this is none other than God himself. Thus Samuel hears the call of the Lord, but doesn't realize what it is (1 Samuel 3:1-18). He has to be told that this is the Lord who has spoken to him (1 Samuel 3:8-10). To take another famous example, Saul of Tarsus has a remarkable experience on the road to Damascus (Acts 9:1-6), but has to be told who it is that had met him on that road: 'I am Jesus, whom you are persecuting' (Acts 9:5). Many people have had the experience of encountering someone or something which they know is real in their personal experience, yet need to be told that this is none other than the living God. And then they start to find out more about him.

This point needs to be remembered in relation to the endless—and remarkably unproductive—arguments about whether the existence of God can be proved. Like a rather tedious game of chess, some of these arguments usually end in a permanent stalemate. Anyhow, it's important to realize that there's a difference between constructing a totally watertight argument for the existence of God and being convinced that

God exists. Many of the world's greatest philosophers think that God's existence can be proved without any real difficulty, but ultimately God's existence doesn't depend upon these arguments. Being convinced that God exists may come about through a variety of factors—such as personal religious experience, reading Scripture, or reflection upon the resurrection—of which rational argument is only one.

In the end, however, the Christian's faith in God doesn't depend upon any argument but upon an experience. This is not to say that no reasons for the existence of God may be given, of course. It is simply to point out that a lot of people have the idea that you have to prove that God exists before you can start taking him seriously, or experience or encounter him. As most of these arguments about whether God exists or not often end in this permanent stalemate, both the atheist and the Christian alike take their positions as a matter of faith. It is worth emphasizing this point, because it is too often overlooked. The atheist believes that there is no God, but his position is a matter of faith rather than fact. He cannot prove beyond all reasonable doubt that God does not exist, just as the Christian cannot prove with total conviction that God does exist: both are positions of faith. Any philosophy of life which is based upon the belief that there is no God (such as Marxism in its many forms) is as much a matter of faith as Christianity itself.

We could take this point a little further. As we shall see later, one of the reasons why Christians believe in God is their conviction that he has revealed himself, supremely in Jesus Christ. This ground of faith in God is in addition to any argument which may possibly prove God's existence. But the atheist's position is based solely upon such arguments—after all, if there is no God, the possibility of this non-existent God actively revealing his non-existence is somewhat remote. Atheism is, in fact, no more 'scientific' than Christian faith, despite the attempts of atheists to convince us otherwise. Both atheism and Christianity are, then, matters of faith—whereas agnosticism is just a matter of indifference.

A number of arguments have been used by atheists in the

present century to attempt to discredit Christianity. None of them is particularly convincing, although some are quite important in terms of their influence. In the following pages we shall examine two of the main arguments for atheism currently in fashion.

1. God is a projection of human ideals and desires

This idea is particularly associated with the early nineteenth-century thinker Ludwig Feuerbach, who is known to have influenced Karl Marx. According to Feuerbach, 'God' is basically nothing more than the projection of human ideals and desires onto an imaginary plane. In other words, we 'project' our desire for eternal life, meaning, love and so forth *ad infinitum*, and call the imaginary result 'God'. God doesn't really exist—but we do. To use the technical Hegelian language which Feuerbach employs to develop this theme: 'God' is the *objectification* of our own desires and longings. Thus whereas orthodox Christianity has always argued that 'God is love' (1 John 4:8), Feuerbach argues that 'love is God', meaning that the human ideal of love is objectified to give the idea of God.

Developing these ideas, Feuerbach argues that atheism is the only way of liberating human beings from their delusion. If only we would realize that there is no God, we could recognize that it is we ourselves who are God—because it is our ideals and desires which we mistakenly think of as God. For this reason, Feuerbach argues that atheism is the true basis of humanism. In order to value humanity properly, it is necessary to deny the existence of God.

This argument was remarkably influential in some circles in the nineteenth and twentieth centuries. For instance, Sigmund Freud's dismissal of religion as some sort of 'wish-fulfilment' is simply a psychological adaptation of Feuerbach's ideas. However, it is clear that there are certain outstanding difficulties with this view, the most obvious being: how can Feuerbach *prove* that his account of how we think of God is right? Basically, Feuerbach is arguing that we invent God because we need him. But this is just a hypothesis, a suggestion, which—by its very nature—cannot be proved. The suggestion that 'God exists because Christians want him to' is just as logically plausible as the suggestion that 'God doesn't exist because atheists don't want him to'. This is no *proof* that God doesn't exist, it is simply an *assertion* that he doesn't.

A second difficulty to be noted is that Feuerbach's argument for atheism seems to rest on a rather elementary logical error. Feuerbach's argument, as has often been observed, runs like this:

(1) Nothing exists, or needs to exist, just because we want it to exist.

(2) We want God to exist.

(3) Therefore God doesn't exist.

The conclusion just doesn't follow from the premises—it is an excellent example of a *non sequitur*. Things don't exist just because we want them to—but from the fact that we *do* desire their existence, it hardly follows that they *don't* exist! The correct conclusion is simply that God cannot be proved to exist just because we want him to exist.

Furthermore, it is absurdly simplistic to think that the existence of God can be regarded simply as a consolation in life, something which makes things easier for us to bear. Time and time again, Scripture represents God as making considerable demands of us, even the surrender of our lives. The historical fact that there have been so many Christian martyrs who knew that God was calling them to lay down their lives for him, should alert us to the naïvety of this argument. This God isn't the sort of sugar-coated God we might like to dream up. As we saw a moment ago, the same faulty logic can lead to the following argument:

(1) Nothing does not exist, nor needs not to exist, just because we don't want it to exist.

(2) Atheists don't want God to exist.

(3) Therefore God exists.

Wishful thinking is hardly the most reliable guide on the basis of which to decide whether God exists or not.

Similarly, Freud's version of the argument simply adds psychological theory to the 'projection theory' which he uncritically accepted as correct. Yet, like Feuerbach, all that Freud succeeds in doing is establishing as a hypothesis the suggestion that religion is an illusion based upon neurosis or immaturity—and proof for this hypothesis is wanting. According to Freud, religious ideas are the fulfilment of the oldest, strongest and most powerful wishes of humanity—but that doesn't mean that religion is a delusion. Simply because we want something to exist, we can hardly conclude that it doesn't exist. And here, of course, Christian theology has a major insight to bear: we are created in the image of God (Genesis 1:26-27), so that some sort of correspondence between our wishes and reality in relation to God *is to be expected*. Freud, of course, had no time for what Christianity had to say on the matter: historically, his own atheism was well established before he developed his psychological theory of religion to support it. It wasn't as if he gave up Christianity because of his psychology—rather, he shaped his psychology to buttress his rejection of Christianity. But logic and theology alike allow the Christian to treat his dismissal of God with exactly the same lack of respect which he himself earlier showed for Christianity.

Finally, a more pragmatic point may be made. Feuerbach was writing in the early nineteenth century at a time when optimism in human nature and potential was considerable. The development of evolutionary theory later that century heightened this optimism. For Feuerbach, man is his own God, and atheism provides a means by which he may be liberated from the false God of Christianity. But Feuerbach did not foresee the horrors of the First World War, of Auschwitz, of human atrocities against fellow humans on a larger scale and with an intensity hitherto undreamed of. More than a century of experience with this man-turned-God demonstrates that he is simply not capable of the responsibilities which being God lays upon him. Having 'liberated' ourselves from one God, we find ourselves enslaved to another lesser God of much more questionable moral character. This pragmatic point confirms the theoretical weakness of Feuerbach's atheism by drawing attention to its practical consequences.

What remains of this atheist argument for the non-existence of God? Not much. Christians can hardly be expected to give up their faith in God just because of an unproven and unprovable suggestion, which ultimately rests upon an elementary logical error, and ignores Christian insights into both God and ourselves. The atheist argument is no proof for the non-existence of God: like arguments for the existence of God, it is at best merely suggestive (how suggestive being a matter for some debate) and most emphatically not conclusive. Not to believe in God on the basis of this argument requires a leap of faith at least as great as that involved in believing that he does exist through the argument from design. In fact, Feuerbach's real significance lies in the influence he had upon the atheism of Karl Marx, to which we now turn.

2. God is the opiate of the masses, serving the vested interests of society

Karl Marx's critique of Christianity has had a powerful influence upon both secular and Christian Western thought, but has not itself been subjected to the rigorous criticism that it so obviously needs. Earlier, we noted Feuerbach's idea that 'God' was the projection of our desires and ideals. Marx develops a slightly different but clearly related idea: our religious ideas, such as God, result from our social and economic situation. In other words, it is the nature of society itself—its social conditions and the economic system which supports it—which governs our thinking about God and so forth.

For Marx, Western European society was the product of the capitalist economic system. This system, particularly the privatization of property, deprived individuals of their proper social rights—it *alienated* them, to use Marx's key term. That alienation has a number of consequences, according to Marx, and one of them is religious belief in God. Faith in God is thus one result of unjust social conditions—and if those conditions are changed, faith in God can, in principle, be eliminated. Underlying Marx's communist vision is a fundamentalist atheism—the uncritical and dogmatic assertion that the coming revolution will eliminate religious belief along with unjust social conditions.

Rejecting the view that there is anything inherently wrong with humanity that causes self-centredness or 'egoism', to use Marx's term, Marx argues that it is capitalism which is the source of humanity's problems. Eliminate capitalism, and human alienation, and hence religion, is eliminated with it. Through socio-economic engineering, the human dilemma may be overcome. At this point, it is worth noticing how Marx locates the problem at the social rather than the individual level—it is society which must be changed if the individual is to be liberated.

Marx thus regards Christianity as the 'opium of the people': a means of alleviating the social misery of the oppressed masses (and hence delaying the inevitable revolution) which is a direct result of their social and economic conditions. Once those socio-economic conditions are altered through the communist revolution, there will no longer be any need for Christianity: it will become redundant.

However, Marx never shows any interest in Christianity as such—he is simply concerned with the social function of religion, whether it is Judaism or Christianity. At no point do we find Marx attempting to criticize any specific doctrines of Christianity or its claims to truth in general: his criticism is based upon his understanding of religion as at best a symptom of human alienation, and at worst a way in which the status quo can be maintained by oppression. Thus Marx's hostility to Christianity occasionally appears to derive from his observation of the behaviour of certain pastors whom he regarded as oppressing the masses, rather than any attempt to come to terms with what Christianity itself has to say.

Marx's criticisms of Christianity never penetrate, or even make the slightest attempt to penetrate, to the essence of the Christian faith. Religion is at best useless and at worst positively harmful, Marx asserts ('argues' is hardly the right word) —and as Christianity is a religion, these criticisms apply to it. We find no attempt to wrestle with the question of the identity of Jesus Christ, or the relevance of the cross and resurrection to the world. Christianity is to be rejected because it stands in the way of Marx's vision of the communist society. It delays the inevitable revolution. For Marx, socialism was an historical inevitability, therefore the elimination of Christianity was equally inevitable—but, as with so many early nineteenth-century theories, the gulf between theory and reality proved to be unbridgable. The passage of time causes the late twentieth-century reader to have the most serious doubts concerning the reliability of Marx's social judgements, let alone the religious views he based upon them. The 'historical inevitability of socialism' has been discredited by much recent social scientific research.

The view of Christianity as opium handed out to the masses by their masters to dull their awareness of their situation—paralleling the modern situation in which psychiatric patients are heavily sedated to prevent them from becoming troublesome in hospital—was developed by Lenin (Vladimir Ilyich Ulyanov). Lenin's absurdly hostile attitude to Christianity as a 'spiritual intoxicant' is based on his conviction that Christianity deceives workers and inhibits the communist revolution. Only by eliminating Christianity and establishing an atheist state may communism be achieved.

We now have enough information about the Marxist critique of Christianity to indicate its obvious weaknesses. First, it is clear that Marx does not directly criticize the specific doctrines of Christianity, such as the existence of God, or the Christian understanding of what God is like. Religion in general, and Christianity in particular, is to be criticized on account of its social functions. The existence of God is not disproved—it is simply declared to be an obstacle to the achievement of Marx's political and economic vision. The plausibility of that vision is itself seriously called into question by the simple fact that Marx's vision of a religionless society is increasingly being recognized as utopian. The fundamental dogma that religion is the consequence of social alienation is seriously undermined by the all-too-obvious fact that religion is nowhere in decline in communist societies. In an effort to make theory and reality converge, forcible suppression of Christianity has been attempted within such societies, but is increasingly being recognized as counterproductive. Even in these societies, human beings remain the fundamentally sinful human beings they always have been and always will be, with human self-interest proving totally resistant to the social cures offered.

Marxism is an example of the countless theories which try to account for the tragic history and situation of humanity in terms of the influence of some external factor—social or economic conditions, poor education, or sexual repression, to give some obvious examples. But is it not the reality that there is some fatal flaw within human nature itself; that there is something inherently wrong with us, which no amount of tampering with external matters will alter? Marxism, like so many other failed remedies of the past for the human predicament, confuses causes and effects, leaving the real source of human misery untouched—and the real source of that misery lies within us, as human beings. It is here that Christianity addresses a fundamental challenge to Marxism, arguing that it is the regeneration and renewal of humanity which is needed if the *real* source of alienation is to be dealt with at its root. Like an amateur physician, Marxism deals with a symptom, thinking it is the disease itself.

What remains of the Marxist criticism of Christianity? Perhaps the important insight that all too often the church has uncritically supported the ruling classes, ignoring its responsibilities to the poor and oppressed. That, however, remains a criticism of how Christianity is applied, rather than of Christianity itself. The church needs to be challenged, both from inside and outside its bounds, to demonstrate that it has social and ethical relevance and does not merely buttress those who exercise power. Marx, however, consistently demonstrated the most superficial understanding of Christianity throughout his life, criticizing Christianity on account of its social role rather than its specific beliefs. The non-existence of God is simply treated as an axiom, a self-evident proposition, by Marx, and is nowhere backed up by arguments which can be thought of as proofs. For Marx, God does not exist in a socialist society, and does not need to exist. But, as history has shown, no amount of socio-economic engineering has achieved the voluntary and self-evident atheism Marx presupposes. It is all too obvious that God will outlive his morticians, Freudian and Marxist alike.

God, then, has taken something of a battering in the last two centuries or so. But, in the words of William Cullen Bryant: 'Truth crushed to earth will rise again.' The alleged 'proofs' of the non-existence of God turn out to be like spiders' webs which collapse when touched, despite looking so attractive and permanent in the early morning mist. For the Christian, the living God is present and active in his world, quite irrespective of whether his existence is recognized or denied. In the end, the Christian doesn't believe in God because someone has argued him into believing that he's there, but because he has experienced, has encountered, the reality of the living God. In the following chapter, we're going to develop this point further.

2

Encountering God

Most people approach Christianity with preconceptions which prevent them from realizing what it's all about in the first place. One of these preconceptions is that you have to believe in God already before Christianity makes any sort of sense. Underlying this is the idea that Christianity basically concerns knowledge about God: given that he exists, we can say this and that about him. But all that this leads to is a *conception* of God, an *idea* about him. When reading history books (as almost all of us are forced to do at some stage in our lives!) we can begin with the assumption that Admiral Nelson or George Washington or Napoleon Bonaparte existed, and go on to find out more about them. And much the same idea persists about Christianity: you start from the assumption that God exists, and then go on to find out something about him by reading the appropriate textbooks, such as the Bible.

What sort of arguments might be advanced to suggest that the assumption that God exists is reasonable? Before we even ask this question, however, it is worth pointing out that for many people, this whole business is a waste of time. God is there, and that's all there is to it. He is experienced as being present and real. Why bother trying to prove that God is there when we already know this from our experience of him? After all, no scriptural writer bothers to give proof of God's exist-ence, of which they were all only too aware. These points must be conceded. But in reply it may be pointed out that these arguments are not directed to those who already know and experience God as a personal reality, but to those who are finding difficulty with the idea of God in the first place. To some, they are helpful starting-points in their thinking about God, and they are useful for that very reason. In what follows, we shall briefly outline three lines of reasoning which point to the existence of God. We shall call these 'the argument from morality', 'the argument from rationality', and 'the argument from desire'.

1. The argument from morality

All of us make moral judgements at times. Even if we find moral philosophy hopelessly bewildering, there are times when we are forced to make judgements about what is right and what is wrong. When the first photographs of what had happened at the concentration camp at Auschwitz were re-leased to an unsuspecting world, most people were sincerely horrified and outraged at what had taken place. They just knew it was wrong intuitively, without the need for any moral guidelines or arguments. But where do these intuitive moral ideas come from? And are they valid, of any significance, to understanding what is right and what is wrong? Or are they simply instincts from the distant past, or inhibitions which arise from society—both of which, when recognized for what they are, may be overcome? After all, we overcome other inhibitions when they get in the way of what we want to do.

However, the simple fact is that we don't regard the ex-ecutioners of Auschwitz as having overcome inhibitions or as having liberated themselves from the primitive forces of in-stinct—we believe, quite forcefully, that they did something which is *wrong*, something which quite definitely ought not to have been done. Similarly, some would argue that 'right' means 'in accord with the laws of the land'. Yet all of us know only too well that laws can be unjust, can be wrong. The executioners of Auschwitz were, after all, acting legally in what they did—yet that hardly makes what they did 'right'. Again, some would argue that the basis of morality is 'the greatest good of the greatest number'. And the executioners of Auschwitz would agree: they were simply liquidating minority groups such as the Jews in order that the well-being of the majority would be enhanced. And so we could go on through the various 'naturalist' explanations of morality. But in the end they fail to satisfy us because they all carry with them the suggestion that morality is arbitrary, something which humans have invented.

Deeply embedded in human nature are ideas of 'right' and 'wrong' which cannot be explained away in this manner. It is almost as if there are certain definite ideas about the way in which we ought and ought not to behave built into human nature. But where do they come from? What lies behind these natural ideas of 'right' and 'wrong'? Perhaps it is nothing— simply the blind and irrational forces of evolution. In which case morality is the law of the jungle, the instinct for survival, and it is robbed of its force. In this view, 'right' and 'wrong' are simply biological behaviour patterns. But the picture is actually more complex than this. Knowing what is right, we often do what is wrong. All of us, when we attempt to live up to our moral ideals (wherever these ideals come from in the first place), find ourselves unable to do so. We *recognize* them, but cannot *actualize* them. There seems to be something about human nature which allows us to recognize what is right, and yet at the same time causes us to fail to do it.

The ability of the Christian understanding of both God and human nature to explain these observations will be obvious. God is the ground and basis of the moral order, the one who created human beings in his own image (Genesis 1:26-27). We should therefore expect some traces of the mind of God to remain stamped upon us as part of our nature. Yet, through sin, our ability to live up to the moral law is compromised (Romans 7:15-25 is worth reading at this point). It is through the realization that we know what is right, and yet are unable to achieve it, that we begin to understand the need for redemption. The coherence of the Christian understanding of God and human nature—which is not based upon such arguments in the first place—is remarkable.

2. The argument from rationality

In assessing whether God exists or not, we are obliged to use our minds, to use reason. This is the tool we regard as appropriate for the task in hand. The reliability of reason to determine whether God exists or not is an inevitable assumption of any argument about whether God exists or not. But this assumption actually implies far more than might at first be thought. Let us suppose that you programme a computer to analyse various pieces of data, and arrive at a conclusion—perhaps to determine the estimated population growth of a country from recent census returns. The accuracy of the relation between the data and the conclusion is determined totally by the way in which you program the computer. Program the computer at random, and the results are unreliable, to say the least. Confidence in the ability of the computer to handle data is ultimately confidence in the computer program, and hence the programmer. If an army of monkeys were to be given access to personal computers, there is a genuine possibility (however slight!) that, given enough time and enough monkeys, one of them would write a program which could handle such data reliably. But it is still very improbable. A good program results from a good programmer.

In turning to deal with the human mind, we are faced with a similar situation. Without pressing the similarity between the mind and a computer too far, it will be obvious that we are faced with a comparable situation—the ability to handle data in order to reach a conclusion. But what is the basis of our trust in reason to do this? It is obvious that all knowledge depends upon the validity of our reasoning process, and any elements of irrationality at any stage in that process of reasoning could potentially invalidate it. It is possible that human reason came into existence by chance, perhaps through the blind forces of evolution, in much the same way as an army of monkeys might write a computer program. Alternatively, we might suggest that underlying *our* reason is *somebody else's* reason, in much the same way as human intelligence lies behind a good computer program. Earlier, we noticed how the Christian understanding of human nature assumed a direct continuity between God and ourselves—and what is true in the field of morality is also true in the field of rationality. Human rationality derives from the divine rationality, and its ability to understand nature is ultimately a reflection of the fact that both were created by the same rational God.

Once more, it is necessary to point out that this doesn't prove that God exists. It simply points out that there is a coherent Christian understanding of the basis of rationality which is perfectly adequate to deal with what we know by experience. It is suggestive, not conclusive.

3. The argument from desire

Most of us are aware of experiences of longing, of desire, for something which requires satisfaction. Hunger is an experience which we all know, and it corresponds to a physiological need within us and something which is objective outside us (food). The feeling of thirst is a parallel case: something natural within us points to a need which can be met by the appropriate external substance (water). A similar point could be made in relation to sexual desire. All these longings within us correspond to a real human need which may be satisfied. Our very survival depends upon these longings pointing beyond themselves to something which may satisfy them. It reflects our physiological make-up, the way we are.

A further deep longing within most individuals is well known, but difficult to put into words. Perhaps its most eloquent analysis may be found in the writings of C. S. Lewis, especially his famous sermon 'The Weight of Glory'. It is a deep longing for something which no finite object can ever satisfy: a spiritual restlessness, a desire for immortality, a search for meaning—we could extend this list at great length. The basic feeling is, however, known to most of us, even if we find it difficult to describe. It is a sense of spiritual emptiness, an awareness that physical things cannot satisfy part of our nature. This feeling is well known to many, and existentialist philosophers have glorified it with the rather clumsy label 'thrown-out-ness'. It is as if we are all in a 'distant country' (Luke 15:13), cut off from a joy which we have never really known, yet which we somehow seem to remember. It is like the echo of a tune which we have never really heard, or news from a country which we have never visited yet which we feel that we somehow already know. But what does this longing point to?

It is, of course, possible to argue that it points to nothing, being simply a by-product of evolution. It might be pointed out in reply that this would be to dismiss or invalidate an alarming number of human emotions. The Christian would say that this deep-felt longing within human nature is a consequence of the way we are made. We are created, as we have seen, in the image of God, with an inbuilt capacity to relate to God; and these spiritual longings within us point to the absence of that relationship. As Pascal put it, 'There is a God-shaped gap within us'—a gap which really exists and which nothing except God himself can fill. Just as hunger points to the need for food, so these spiritual longings point to the need for God. The full force of this point is obvious to Christians, who find it virtually impossible to think of life without God. Without God, there would be an emptiness, a void, in human existence of such magnitude that life would hardly seem worth living. But even for the non-Christian, the force of this point should be clear. Unless we are to invalidate our experiences, we must ask what this sense of spiritual emptiness means. Perhaps it means nothing and is insignificant; perhaps it is pointing towards a real need which can be met by none other than the living God; perhaps it is pointing towards our spiritual homeland, the distant country, to which we are being called home.

At this point, it is worth noting how often Scripture compares experiencing God with satisfying physical needs. 'Taste and see that the Lord is good,' says the Psalmist (Psalm 34:8).

Jesus Christ is variously referred to as the 'bread of life' or 'the living water'. 'I am the bread of life. He who comes to me will never go hungry, and he who believes in me will never be thirsty' (John 6:35); 'Whoever drinks the water I give him will never thirst' (John 4:14). The awareness of spiritual hunger and thirst, by analogy with physical hunger and thirst, raises the question of whether this hunger and thirst may be satisfied —and Christianity proclaims that they may indeed be more than satisfied through an encounter with the living God.

Once more, it is necessary to point out that such an argument is suggestive rather than conclusive. But here, as with the other two arguments, it is worth noticing how the Christian understanding of the relation of God and ourselves ties in perfectly with experience. Faith illuminates experience, and is in turn validated by experience. Christianity interprets our experiences in terms of the need to enter into a relationship with God, and proclaims that this relationship is a real possibility through the death and resurrection of Jesus Christ.

What is the relevance of arguments such as these, which suggest that God exists but do not prove it? Ultimately, the only meaningful proof is encounter with and experience of God as the reality towards which such considerations point. Let us illustrate this point by considering two similar situations, both concerning the heavens, one drawn from the New Testament and the other from the world of astronomy.

As even the most casual reader of the New Testament and practically everyone who sends or receives Christmas cards knows, shortly after his birth Jesus was visited by the wise men, the mysterious night visitors from the East (Matthew 2:1-12). (Actually, we don't know how many of them there were, even though the traditional number is three. What we do know is that they brought three gifts (Matthew 2:11), and we always assume that they brought one each!) What was it that brought them to Jesus? All too often the impression is given that the wise men, who were almost certainly the astronomers of their day, were led directly to Bethlehem by the appearance of the famous star, whereas what actually happened was rather different. They saw the star at its rising, which alerted them to the existence of a new-born king, and travelled to Jerusalem in order to be given more specific directions; and it was from Jerusalem that they were directed to Bethlehem. An event in the world of nature—the star—led them to begin the search for the Messiah, and took them part of the way to finding him. But for the final part of that search, they relied upon the great Old Testament prophecies as to where this individual would be born (Matthew 2:2-8). Scripture confirmed what nature suggested—that the new-born king was to be found in Bethlehem.

The parallel with arguments for the existence of God will be obvious. Like the star of Bethlehem, they point to something, but do not take us all the way; they indicate the existence of something, but do not disclose exactly what it is or where it may be found. The important thing is to go on from there, inquiring as to where God may be found. Like the wise men, we too are led to Scripture if we are to find out more about this God and where he may be found. And, as Christianity has always insisted, God is most reliably to be found and known in precisely the same place in which those wise men first found him—in the person of Jesus Christ. Arguments for the existence of God, like the star of Bethlehem, can bring us part of the way to finding God, but for the final part of that journey we need guidance from those who already know where he may be found, or who have already found him. We shall return to this point shortly. Let us turn from the star of Bethlehem to another, more recent, event relating to our knowledge of the heavens.

In the year 1781, the English astronomer, William Herschel, caused considerable excitement by discovering the mysterious green planet, Uranus. Up to this point it had been generally assumed that the entire solar system was already known, and the discovery of this mysterious new member of the solar system called many of the traditional presuppositions about that system into question. By the year 1820, however, it was observed that this new planet behaved in an unusual way. Its orbit was not exactly what was expected. Several explanations were advanced to explain these perturbations to its

orbit: perhaps the planet Saturn was heavier than had generally been assumed, or perhaps there was a still unknown
planet lying beyond Uranus which was distorting its orbit
through gravitational attraction. It was far from clear exactly
how the evidence was to be interpreted, but it was certainly
highly suggestive.

In 1843, John Couch Adams at Cambridge and August
Leverrier at Paris began to explore the hypothesis that there
was a trans-Uranic planet. Although it had not been seen and
recognized by anyone up to this point, they were able to work
out roughly where this planet should be found in the night
sky. In England and in Berlin, telescopes began to search the
skies for this hypothetical planet—until the Berlin observ-
atory finally reported its discovery. The new planet was
named Neptune. In due course, it was found that perturbations to the orbit of this new planet suggested the existence
of a planet lying still further from the sun, eventually leading
to the discovery of Pluto in 1930.

The point we want to make is obvious. On the basis of data
which suggested, but did not prove, the existence of a planet
lying beyond Uranus, the search for this planet was under-
taken with seriousness and commitment, eventually leading to
its discovery. So it is with God. The evidence for his existence
is real and highly suggestive, but not conclusive. The existence
of God is one possible way of explaining the evidence of experience, but not the only way. Just as the trans-Uranic-planet
hypothesis was only finally verified by taking it seriously, and
looking for that planet where the evidence suggested it might
be found, so the 'God hypothesis' can be verified by taking it
seriously and looking for him where Christianity has always
suggested he may be found. And where is God to be found?
Like the planet Neptune, in the night sky? Perhaps (see
Psalms 8:3; 19:1). But the Christian points to the biblical
record culminating in Jesus Christ, especially in his death and
resurrection, as the supreme demonstration of the existence
and character of God. It is here that Christianity has always
insisted that God is most reliably disclosed and revealed: it is
here that he may be found. To develop this point, let us con-

sider how the biblical witness to God both confirms and extends any knowledge of God available from nature itself.

An example may help to make this point clearer. The idea that God is the creator of the world in which we live, including ourselves, is often argued by some philosophers to be obvious from nature itself. This theme is familiar to most readers of classical philosophical works. On the other hand, as Cicero pointed out in his *De natura deorum* ('On the nature of the gods'), the ideas of God which were obtained from nature were fragmentary and often inconsistent. There was a limit to what could be known about God from nature—for example, that he was the creator, and that he was good and wise. This point was developed further in the eighteenth century by Bishop Butler in his famous work *The Analogy of Religion*. Butler underscored the ambiguity of nature as a source of knowledge of God: after all, nature was littered with violence, waste and carnage; 'red in tooth and claw', and with the moral code 'eat or be eaten', it was hardly the best place to look for God! If reliable knowledge of God is to be had, a more reliable source than nature is required.

At this point, the Christian will point out that Scripture endorses these insights drawn from nature—for example, that God is the creator, and that he is good and wise—as well as developing them. There is a hymn by Isaac Watts which deserves to be known better than it is:

> The heavens declare thy glory, Lord!
> In every star thy wisdom shines;
> But when our eyes behold thy word,
> We read thy name in fairer lines.

The basic point being made is that the scriptural witness to God is consistent with and endorses what we already know, or think we know, by experience, and that it both states this more clearly and develops it further. Scripture establishes a reliable framework for thinking and talking about God, which goes far beyond the very modest knowledge of God which it is possible to derive from nature. And Scripture constructs this framework around the central event to which it bears witness:

the life, death and resurrection of Jesus Christ.

The importance of the scriptural testimony in relation to any discussion of God which claims to be *Christian* cannot be overestimated. We need to be told what God is like—left to ourselves we would just end up with a bewildering and contradictory collection of ideas about what God might be like. Scripture authorizes us to talk about God in certain very definite ways: it lays down the framework for our discussion of God. As we shall see in later chapters, it is Scripture which bears witness to God as he has revealed himself to us. Christians have always recognized that they are responding to God's revelation of himself, and not just inventing ideas about who God is and what he might be like. God's revelation of himself, culminating in the death and resurrection of Jesus Christ, is mediated to us through the scriptural testimony. And so it is Scripture which is the primary source of Christian reflection on who God is and what he is like. As we have seen, the scriptural witness to God ties in with experience—but it goes far beyond it, adding important insights which otherwise we could not hope to have.

Thinking about God is difficult for many people because it seems terribly abstract. We can't see, hear or touch God in the way that we can experience other objects around us. Often we feel that we need something more concrete, more tangible, on which to base our discussion of God. One of the most powerful insights which the Christian religion has to offer concerns the way in which we know about God in the first place. According to Christianity, the most reliable knowledge of God which we have in this life is to be found in the person of Jesus Christ. In *Understanding Jesus*, I spent some time exploring this very important insight, and we shall return to this point in later chapters. But the history of Jesus is also of importance in connection with the question of the existence of God. The resurrection of Jesus immediately forces us to ask: who or what lay behind this remarkable event?

As we saw in *Understanding Jesus*, the first Christians were completely convinced that the resurrection did not merely demonstrate the existence of God, but represented God's endorsement of Jesus' mission. His words and deeds were, so to speak, stamped with the seal of divine approval through the resurrection. The resurrection overturned the judgement of the world—that Jesus was a failure—and established in its place the judgement of God upon all that Jesus said and did. The resurrection demonstrated that God endorsed and vindicated Jesus, whereas the world had thought God condemned him. Important though the resurrection is in answering the question of exactly who Jesus was, and why he is so important, we must realize that the resurrection is also of importance in relation to our knowledge of God. For the Christian, the existence of God is confirmed by the resurrection of Jesus Christ.

This point is also of relevance to those who find arguments about the existence of God hopelessly abstract. Instead of thinking about abstract ideas like morality or reason, we can start thinking about something very specific and very definite: exactly what was it that happened on the first Easter Day? What was it that transformed the experience of the disciples? What was the meaning of the empty tomb? These are all historical questions, not abstract philosophical questions. The Christian answer is that God raised Jesus Christ from the dead. Alternative explanations seem so improbable that we are continually forced back to the Christian answer as the most satisfying. The reality of God is expressed in the transformation of the situation of Good Friday into the situation of Easter Day, in which death gave way to new life, despair to joy, and darkness to light. And in the same way the gospel holds out the promise of the transformation of our own situation here and now. The same God who raised Jesus Christ from the dead makes himself available for us, promising to transform our death to new life, our despair to joy, our darkness to light. And the Christian experience of God is that he has done and still does precisely this to those who come to him.

These lines of argument, however, may suggest that the only way to become a Christian is to arrive at belief in the existence of God, and then go on to ask what extra facts

Christianity has to add to this belief. In fact, this is not correct. To go back to our history book analogy, the Christian view of God is best compared to a historical figure who steps out of the pages of a history textbook and meets us right where we are. The idea that we have to discover who God is, and what he is like, is quite foreign to Christianity, which is based on the recognition that God has taken the initiative and come to meet us in history. What is offered to us is not just information about God, but the living God himself. This point is very important, and we shall explore it a little further before moving on to other matters.

Many people seem to think that a precondition for becoming a Christian is belief in God, and that Christianity just supplements this belief by adding one or two extra bits to this basic belief such as ideas about how we should behave, and so on. In fact, most people seem to disregard or reject Christianity on the basis of what they think it ought to be about, rather than what Christianity actually has to say. But Christians don't think in this way. They don't think of themselves as *searching for God*—they think of themselves as *having been found by God*, waiting for the God who comes to them. Both the Old and the New Testaments speak of a God who seeks us out, who comes to meet us where we are and take us home with him. The Bible inverts the scheme many of us are used to working with—our search for God—and invites us to think instead of God's search for us. God comes to search for us, to meet us where we are, to make himself available for our acceptance or our rejection. It is this step which many find difficult to take, largely because they are still working with the idea of God as a concept, something which exists in the world of ideas. Christians, as I emphasize throughout this book, work with the idea of God as a person, some*one* (not some*thing*) who is able to take the initiative in making himself known to us and establishing a relationship with us.

To encounter God is to encounter a personal reality, not just to have an interesting (if unoriginal) idea. The idea of God needs to be supplemented by a personal encounter with the living God to which it points and bears witness. For some people the idea of God is an end in itself, whereas for the Christian it is one possible starting-point for the real objective —a personal relationship with the living and loving God. Thus Christian faith is not so much about *belief* in the *idea* of God, as *trust* in the *person* of God. Of course, it is obvious that we can't dispense with the idea of God—and nobody is suggesting for one moment that we could. The point we're trying to make is that the Christian experience of God is infinitely more rich and profound than a mere idea!

Let us take this one stage further. We can encounter a person of whose existence we were quite unaware up to that point. Every now and then, you come across a magazine article or news item about someone being reunited with a long-lost brother or sister of whose existence they were quite unaware. You may read about someone, such as the President of the United States, and then meet him—but all of us know that it is perfectly normal to meet someone whom we have never heard of before. After all, that's how many friendships develop. And so it is with God. It is not just possible, but positively routine, for individuals to meet God, to encounter him, even though they hadn't believed in him previously. Just as a new and hitherto unknown person may suddenly enter into our lives, so God is able to do exactly the same.

Encounter with God and belief in God's existence may come about simultaneously. It is part and parcel of the Christian experience of God that he acts in this way. It may be that this encounter with God is not recognized for what it really is—and the case of Samuel may be noted again (1 Samuel 3:1-10)—but there are remarkably few individuals who have not, at some time in their lives, felt something strange, something awesome, something disturbing, something inexplicable, at work within them, challenging their perceptions of reality and enlarging their mental horizons. This feeling, deeply embedded in human religious experience down the ages, was addressed by Paul in his famous sermon at the Areopagus in Athens (Acts 17:16-34). 'Now what you worship as something unknown I am going to proclaim to you' (Acts 17:23) he declared—in other words, Christianity puts a name to this reality of which we are aware, and opens the way towards a full appreciation of the richness and profundity of the experience of God.

In this chapter, we have been exploring ways in which we come to a knowledge of God. The basic idea is that of a partial and imperfect awareness of the existence and nature of God from nature itself, which is confirmed, supplemented and developed through the scriptural witness, culminating in Jesus Christ. The word of God *was spoken* by the prophets, but the word of God *became incarnate* in Jesus Christ. The same God who spoke through the law and the prophets became like one of us, a mortal and frail human being, in order to speak to us directly. 'In the past God spoke to our forefathers through the prophets at many times and in various ways, but in these last days he has spoken to us by his Son' (Hebrews 1:1-2). Real knowledge of God is not just a list of points about God, but a real and redeeming encounter with the living God, in which God—so to speak—steps out of the pages of Scripture to confront us and challenge us with his presence.

When I was doing research in molecular biology some time ago, there was considerable excitement about the development of new techniques which allowed us to examine animal or plant cells without disturbing them in any way. These techniques were known as 'non-invasive', because they didn't involve disturbing or intruding upon the system being studied. And most people like to work with a 'non-invasive' concept of God—a God who doesn't disturb us or affect us in any way at all. God is treated like a book on a shelf, which may be lifted down when needed, and ignored the rest of the time. John Owen's witty lines, written in the seventeenth century, are still as relevant as ever:

> God and the doctor we alike adore,
> But only when in danger, not before;
> The danger o'er, both are alike requited,
> God is forgotten, and the doctor slighted!

Nobody can be argued into the kingdom of God, for the very reason that Christianity does not concern ideas but a living reality. To persuade someone that God exists is not necessarily to make him a Christian, but for someone to encounter the living God and respond to him—now that is something very different. After all, I could persuade a male friend of mine that a certain female exists—but there is all the difference in the world between that and my friend meeting this girl, discovering that they can relate to each other, and falling in love. Christianity is not like some sort of religious education lesson in which facts are pumped into our heads; rather it is like a love affair—something powerful, challenging and possessing real meaning to those involved. And it is this knowledge of God to which the Christian faith bears witness. It isn't a 'knowledge' for which a relatively high IQ and a university degree are required, but a personal knowledge of God which lies within the grasp of everyone. It is a knowledge which involves our hearts, not just our heads. It is a knowledge which arises through meeting someone, through encountering the living God, not through reading dry and dusty textbooks.

This point is so important that one final illustration will be given. All of us admire someone greatly—it may be an historical figure from the past or someone who is still alive. Suppose you identify one person like this. You could find out a lot about him. You could study all the right books and magazine articles, and listen to all the right TV and radio programmes, and you'd soon know a lot about that person. My approach to Martin Luther, one of my own favourite people, is rather similar. I've read just about everything he wrote, and even more that has been written about him. But Luther is a dead figure from the past, someone whom I will never know as a person, someone with whom I could never establish a personal friendship. It may be the same with the person you're thinking of as well. That person remains someone distant, someone you know a lot about but don't know personally.

Now, imagine there's a knock at your front door, and you discover that the person you admire so much is there, asking to be let in so that he or she can meet you and get to know you. Can you see that there's all the difference in the world between this situation and knowing about the person from books? Now you're meeting a living reality, where before you were just learning facts. You come to know that person in a new, a qualitatively different, way. And so it is with the Christian experience of God. There is a quantum leap between these two ways of knowing someone. If you must, you can learn all about God from books. But the Christian experience of God is that he's knocking at the door of your life, asking to be let in so that he can get to know you and relate to you (Revelation 3:20-22). He isn't breaking the door down with a sledge-hammer, but gives you the privilege of saying no. Real knowledge of God comes about through opening that door and letting him in, and in no other way. Afterwards you read about him in a new light and a new way, because now you can relate to him in a completely different way.

Here, then, is no shallow and superficial textbook knowledge of God, but something vital and dynamic, something exciting, something which gives meaning to life. This is no dead letter, but a living reality. To know God is to encounter the living and loving God, and really to live and really to love as a result. Christianity is about a meeting which becomes a love affair between us and the living God who comes in search of us and takes the initiative in meeting us. The full extent of God's love for us is revealed in the cross of Jesus Christ (John 3:16; Romans 5:8). To be a Christian is to take God's proffered hand and go forwards into eternal life, not quite knowing what this will involve, but being certain that, wherever we go and whatever happens as a result, he will never let us go.

3

Thinking about God

The nineteenth-century poet Tennyson is reported to have
said that most Englishmen pictured God as an enormous
clergyman with a long beard. Whether this is a helpful way of
thinking about God is open to question, but it does draw
attention to the fact that we need to visualize God in some
sort of way. How often have we been reminded that a picture
is worth a thousand words? Some theologians prefer to talk
about God in terms of abstractions, often giving the impression that this is the only respectable way for intelligent
human beings to think about God. Many of us have had to
wade our way through their somewhat turgid discussions of
'the ground of our being', 'ultimate being', and so on, often
not realizing that it is God they're trying to talk about. It is
thus something of a relief to turn back to the world of Scripture, which offers us a series of highly effective pictures of
God (such as God as a father, and God as a shepherd) drawn
from everyday life, building up to give us a comprehensive
view of what God is like. Although none of these images is
adequate in itself, together they give a consistent and satisfying picture of what God is like.

In the next chapter, we'll be looking at these pictures or
models of God, and seeing how, individually and collectively,

they help us think about God. Before we do that, however, we must deal with some questions which arise from using these pictures or models in the first place. Perhaps the most obvious of these is the simple question: why do we need to use these models at all? Why can't we just give an exact description or a precise definition of what God is like, and dispense with all these ideas? After all, they are somewhat elementary, and surely we ought to be able to dispense with them and get on to more sophisticated ways of thinking about God.

The first point that should be noted is human finitude and sinfulness. How can mortal, fallen humans ever expect fully to appreciate or understand what God is really like? When we consider what the word 'God' actually means, it is absurd to suppose that we can ever fully describe or define him. God is someone of whom we catch glimpses, as seen through dark glass (1 Corinthians 13:12, Authorized Version). For the human mind to capture God in his fullness is about as probable as being able to pour the entire Atlantic Ocean into a bucket!

The early fathers of the Christian church used to compare understanding God with looking directly into the sun. The human eye is simply not capable of withstanding the intense light of the sun. And just as the human eye can't cope with the brilliance of the sun, so the human mind can't cope with the glory of God. The well-known words of Bishop Reginald Heber are relevant here:

> Holy, Holy, Holy, though the darkness hide Thee,
> Though the eye of sinful man
> Thy glory may not see.

The story of the pagan emperor who visited the Jewish rabbi Joshua ben Hananiah is also of relevance. The pagan emperor asked to be shown Joshua's god. The rabbi replied that this was impossible, an answer which failed to satisfy the emperor. So the rabbi took the emperor outside and asked him to stare at the midday summer sun. 'Impossible!' replied the emperor. 'If you can't look at the sun, which God created,' replied the rabbi, 'how much less can you behold the glory of God himself.'

As every amateur astronomer knows, however, it is possible to look at the sun through dark glass, or in the early morning through a mist, both of which greatly reduce the brilliance of its disc to manageable proportions. In these ways the human eye can cope with an object which is otherwise completely beyond its capacities. In much the same way, it is helpful to think of the scriptural models or pictures of God as revealing God in manageable proportions so that the human mind can cope with him. The great reformer John Calvin is often thought of as being a rather stern theologian, but he has his tender moments as well. One of those moments lies in his famous assertion that 'God accommodates himself to our weakness'—in other words, God knows the limitations of our intellects and deliberately reveals himself in such a way that we can cope with him.

It is in this respect that the doctrine of the incarnation is of such importance. (See my book *Understanding Jesus*, pp. 91-119, for a discussion of the incarnation and the insights into God which it allows us.) We could say that Jesus is God 'scaled down to size', or in Charles Wesley's famous words, 'our God contracted to a span'. The basic idea is that something or someone who is vast and complex is presented to us in such a way that we can grasp him and begin to make sense of him. God came to us in a way appropriate to our human condition, in the form of something which we could see, touch and handle (see 1 John 1:1-3).

When I was young, I can remember trying to understand what numbers meant. What does the concept of 'three' mean, for example? The way I had to conceptualize 'three' was by looking at three counters, or three chairs, or three tables, and learning that the concept of 'three' was being embodied in each case. As I got used to this way of thinking, I soon learned to think of the idea of 'three' without needing to think about chairs or tables at the same time. And in many ways, this is a helpful way of thinking about the incarnation. Abstract ideas are difficult for us to cope with, and God knows this, and so he reveals himself in a form we can cope with. God reveals himself in the form of a person, in the form of someone whom we can identify with, visualize and relate to. And just as I, when I was young, had to think of 'three' in the specific form of three chairs or three tables, so we learn to think of 'God' in terms of Jesus Christ. To quote the famous words of a second-century writer, 'We must learn to think of Jesus as of God' (1 Clement 1:1). Of course, the incarnation is far more than à way of helping us to grasp truths which would otherwise be difficult or inaccessible, as we saw in *Understanding Jesus*, but one of its several functions is to enable us to begin to think about God in a thrilling and exciting way which would otherwise be denied to us.

In many areas of life we come across the problem of trying to express or portray something rich and profound, and find ourselves seriously restricted by the medium we're using. An obvious example brings this point out very well. Let's suppose that you are out walking one day and come across a magnificent view, a panorama which holds your attention and which you want to record in some permanent form. Back at home, you get your pencil and drawing-pad out and sketch the scene. Immediately you find yourself limited and restricted by having to represent a three-dimensional world on a flat sheet of paper. There is an extra dimension to reality which you simply can't reproduce on the two dimensions of the paper. You may, by skilful use of perspective, manage to create the illusion of a third dimension, but the fact remains that it cannot be captured adequately. And although you may be able to convey shadows and highlights by skilful use of your pencil, the fact remains that you are sketching in black pencil on a white background, producing a monochrome version of a multicoloured reality. Once more, we find it impossible to convey colour adequately through monochrome, even though we may be able to make the best possible use of the materials and techniques we have at our disposal.

So it is with our thinking about God. God has an extra dimension which we cannot really accommodate properly. Just as we cannot adequately convey a multicoloured object in monochrome, so we cannot adequately express God's nature in human words. The Austrian philosopher Ludwig Wittgenstein pointed out that human words were completely incapable of describing something as mundane as the aroma of coffee. How much more difficult it is, then, to describe God! No way of representing God can ever do justice to him as he really is, and we must learn to do the best with what we've got.

Let's develop our sketch-pad analogy further, in order to make an additional important point. Let us suppose that you lived in a dungeon all your life and were cut off from all contact with the outside world. You know nothing of trees, the sun or the sky—all you know about is the dark room in which you've been trapped all your life. Then one day a newcomer arrives in the cell and tells you that there's a world outside that dungeon of which you were hitherto totally unaware. You may have argued that there must be a better world than the one which you already know, but you couldn't be sure. The arrival of this individual with news of this world intrigues and excites you. Perhaps the first question you ask is: what is it like?

In reply, the newcomer takes out a pencil and sketch-pad and starts to draw. He draws a picture of a landscape with sun, trees and sky; he sketches animals, plants and rivers. You are bewildered, for all you see is pencil lines on paper. You find it difficult to understand that you are dealing with a black-and-white, two-dimensional representation of a coloured, three-dimensional reality. The idea that you are being presented with a reduced or scaled-down version of the reality outside your dungeon is virtually impossible for you to comprehend. The breakthrough only really takes place when you realize that the sketches are inadequate and partial representations of a greater reality which itself simply cannot be adequately represented through the medium in question. Of course, if you yourself were able to break free from your dungeon and see the outside world, you'd be able to realize how the sketch related to the reality. But let's suppose you can't break free, and that you remain trapped. Your knowledge of that outside world remains given and embodied in the form of those sketches.

In many ways this analogy captures the situation we find ourselves in as we try to think about and picture God. The basic problem is that we, who have never penetrated beyond our own world of time and space, possess certain highly suggestive insights pointing to the existence of another world lying beyond us. But our knowledge of that world is given to us in the medium of human words—a medium which is the best we possess, but one that cannot portray it adequately. Our knowledge of God takes the form of verbal pictures, of sketches in words. And we must learn that these verbal sketches, while never adequately conveying the glory, majesty and beauty of God, can nevertheless give us an inkling of what he is like, just as the newcomer's pencil sketches would give the inhabitant of the dungeon an idea of what the outside world was like.

This is another way of saying that the medium we are forced to use is inadequate to convey the fullness of both trees and God. A black-and-white sketch of a tree points to what the real thing is like and allows us to identify the real thing when we encounter it. But there is just no way in which those gentle pencil strokes can ever adequately represent every aspect of that tree. Let's consider two situations. Let's suppose that you show this sketch to someone who's seen a tree already. He will recognize your sketch immediately—he shares your experience of a tree and knows what it is that you are drawing. Now suppose you've never seen a tree in your life, like the prisoner in the dungeon. When you encounter a tree for the first time, you realize what it is. You can see the obvious resemblance between the pencil sketch and the real thing.

Similarly, the medium we have to use to describe God is human words. There is just no way that these words can do justice to everything we'd like to say about God. In fact, it's difficult even to know where to start. But what we can do is give a verbal equivalent of a pencil sketch, building up a picture of what God is like. We could use parables, or the sort of models we'll be talking about later in this chapter. And someone who already knows God will recognize that we're talking about the same God that he knows and experiences. Our words ring true to his experience—he can make the connection between our words and his experience.

Now suppose you talk to someone who has never experienced God before. He gets a 'feel' for what God must be like, even though he has never encountered or experienced him. And when he encounters God, he realizes who and what it is that he has encountered. He can make the connection: 'This experience I have just had corresponds to what you were talking about.' The important point here is that although human words are inadequate fully to express the richness and depth of the Christian experience and knowledge of God, they point to God in much the same way as a sketch of a tree points to the tree itself.

We could develop our dungeon analogy still further. Christianity has always insisted that Scripture contains insights into the nature of God which are confirmed and developed through God himself coming to us. In the birth, life, death and resurrection of Jesus Christ we can see God himself coming to us, in our human situation, in much the same way as the newcomer arrived in the dungeon. God 'visits' (see Luke 1:68, Authorized Version) his people, giving them insights concerning himself. Those insights take the form of verbal pictures, models of God in the form of words, which enable us to begin to visualize who God is and what he is like. In addition to these is one picture or model of God which towers over the rest: the person of Jesus Christ, whom faith recognizes to be none other than God incarnate, the living God coming to live among us as one of us.

Now, we have been left these verbal pictures in Scripture and in the memory of the church in order that we may, in our own day and age, begin to think about God on their basis. Of course, they cannot do justice to the reality of the living God, but they point us in the right direction and begin to help us think about God in ways which would otherwise be denied to us. One day, Christians believe that they will see God face to face, as he really is, so that all these partial ways of thinking about him may be left behind for ever. But until that day dawns, we must rely upon the richness of the biblical witness to God, confirmed in Christian experience, as the basis for our thinking about him. We must recognize its limitations, but rejoice that we have these verbal sketches on which to base and build our understanding of who God is and what he is like.

How, then, may we best use these verbal sketches or models of God? We can take our understanding of 'models' of God much further by thinking about the way in which models are used in scientific thinking in order to advance our knowledge of the natural world. For the scientist, models are partial, conceivable ways of imagining or mentally picturing something which is not itself observable. In other words, it is a way of thinking about something which we otherwise have considerable difficulty in visualizing, which allows us to gain insights into the world of nature. In fact, so successful have some of these models become that many people think that they are to be identified with the real thing. This point is so important that we must think about it in more detail, especially for the benefit of anyone who has found this paragraph difficult reading.

Let's begin by thinking about a situation familiar to many people who study science at high school. If you compress gas in a container, you find that the volume the gas occupies gets smaller as the pressure you apply gets greater. This observation, stated in a more mathematical form, is known as Boyle's Law. If you think of the molecules of gas as billiard or pool balls continually bumping in to each other, you find that you can predict this law. The smaller the space in which the billiard balls are forced to move (in other words, the volume), the more they collide with each other and the sides of the container (in other words, they exert more pressure). This model is sometimes known as the kinetic theory of gases.

Now, nobody is saying that gas molecules are identical with billiard balls—for a start, they're billions and billions of times smaller. What we are saying is that billiard balls are a good model for gas molecules, and for two reasons. First, they allow us to picture what molecules are like. We can't see the molecules—they're far too small—but the model allows us to visualize them, to form a mental picture of what they're like. It's not ideal, but it allows us to think of the molecules, to form a picture of them, where otherwise we couldn't picture them at all. Secondly, it allows us to understand and explore at least one aspect of the behaviour of those molecules. Obviously, it doesn't allow us to explain every aspect of their behaviour, but it does help us understand at least part of what's going on, and allow us to try and predict some other properties of the system. It's like an analogy—and we all know that analogies are helpful, providing we remember that every analogy breaks down at some point. And so it is with models—they help us think about things which we otherwise couldn't visualize at all, and allow us to understand at least part of what's going on. Going back to the kinetic theory of gases for a moment, it will be obvious that we are saying that 'the complex behaviour of gases can be partially understood if we think of gas molecules as being like hard inelastic spheres such as billiard or pool balls.'

One of the many interesting things about university Christian groups is that many of their members—indeed, often the majority of their members—are studying natural sciences rather than arts. Why is this? Perhaps one reason might be that they are aware of the handiwork of God as they see it in nature, whereas arts students tend to study the work of other human beings. But perhaps another, and more important consideration is that scientists are used to talking and thinking about reality in terms of models, in terms of partial and conceivable representations of reality, and thus have little difficulty in handling the same tools when speaking and thinking about God.

We could go on and give many more examples of the scientific use of models, but the basic point we're trying to make is clear. It will also be obvious that we use much the same sorts of models to think about God. For example, we could model God on a shepherd, just as we model gas molecules on billiard balls. Here we take something which we are already familiar with and know something about (the shepherd), and say that it gives us a useful mental picture of God, and helps us understand the way in which he behaves. In the following chapter, we'll be looking in some detail at the biblical models of God and what they have to tell us about him. But first, we need to note several important points about models if we are to avoid making some elementary mistakes when we use them.

First, we may accidentally identify the model with what is being modelled. To go back to the kinetic theory, we might accidentally assume that gas molecules *are* billiard balls. Remember, what is being said is that in certain respects gas molecules behave *as if they were* billiard balls. Similarly, when we suggest that a suitable model for God is a shepherd, we are saying that in certain respects God may be thought of as being like a shepherd—for example, in his care for and guidance of his sheep. We must always remember that a model is both like and unlike what is being modelled—the important thing is to identify what the points of likeness are.

It is amazing how many people reject Christianity because they confuse the mental pictures or visual aids with the reality they're trying to describe. These models, however, are not the real thing which Christians believe in—most Christians are only too painfully aware of the enormous difficulties faced in trying to describe God, and are profoundly grateful that God has 'accommodated himself to our weakness' (Calvin) by giving us such helpful and memorable ways of thinking about him. However, we can only use these pictures properly when we understand that they themselves are not what Christians believe, but that Christians believe in God, to whom these pictures point. We may often hear people saying, 'I can't believe in some sort of shepherd up in the sky,' or, 'You can't expect me to take all this nonsense about an old man sitting on a heavenly cloud seriously.' These people, however, are simply confusing a way of picturing God with the reality of God himself. To bring out this crucial point, let's consider another analogy.

Let's suppose that we ask three artists to paint a picture of a bowl of fruit. We invite them into our studio, put a bowl of fruit in front of them, and leave them to get on with it. Later we come back and discover three very different paintings. One is a very straightforward representation of a bowl of fruit, which is immediately recognizable as such. The second is rather more difficult to recognize as a bowl of fruit: all the fruit has inexplicably taken on the shape of cubes, and the colours of the fruit have been transformed into various shades of blue. The third painting is totally unrecognizable: the artist belongs to one of the more abstract schools of interpretation, and the painting vaguely resembles a patchwork quilt. Now, we invite some friends round to look at the paintings. First they look at the third painting, and then we ask them what it represents. After several minutes' baffled silence, we take them to the next painting. Here the silence is shorter, as some of the group begin to see the outlines of the bowl of fruit. When they come to the first painting they have no difficulty in recognizing what is being portrayed—and so when we show them the original bowl of fruit, they have no difficulty in recognizing it as what the first painting was based on.

Let's take this analogy a stage further. Does the fact that the third picture was not recognized as an adequate representation of the bowl of fruit mean that the bowl of fruit didn't exist in the first place, or that it was not a representation of that bowl of fruit? Both of these conclusions are clearly incorrect. We might be tempted to draw them, but they are not logically valid. The only valid conclusion is that the painting was not immediately recognizable as a representation of the reality of the bowl of fruit. Very much the same situation exists with models or visual pictures of God. We may find them difficult to understand, and even be tempted to dismiss them, but this has no bearing whatsoever on the reality which they represent. We could tear up that third painting and consign it to a rubbish bin, but the bowl of fruit would still exist. When dealing with either paintings of bowls of fruit or models of God, therefore, we must avoid confusing the representation of reality with that reality itself.

Secondly, we must remember that complicated things may need more than one model to explain them. An excellent example of this is light. In the early twentieth century it became increasingly clear that the behaviour of light was such that it could only be explained by assuming that certain aspects of that behaviour had to be explained by treating it as a wave, and others by treating it as a particle. In other words, two different (and contradictory) models had to be used if the full complexity of the behaviour of light was to be explained. In fact, a theory was later developed (the famous 'Quantum Theory') which enabled these models to be reconciled. Each of these models illuminated some aspects of the behaviour of light, and failed to clarify others. But they were complementary, rather than contradictory. Broadly speaking, the more complex the situation, the greater the number of models needed to explain it. Every now and then, books with titles such as *Models of Humanity* appear, making it clear just how many different models have to be used even to begin to account for the complexity of human beings. And so when we come to deal with models of God, we should hardly be surprised to find that there are many models given in Scripture, each of which illuminates one aspect of God, and which together combine in a complementary manner to build up a powerful and evocative picture of God.

Thirdly, it may be assumed that something which is necessary for the model is also necessary for whatever is being modelled. We could put this more formally by saying that the logical necessity of some of the features of the model are improperly projected onto the system being modelled. An example will help bring out the relevance of this difficult but important point. In the second half of the nineteenth century it became increasingly clear that light could, in some respects, be treated as if it was a wave motion. One example of wave motion was already well known—sound. Sound was thus treated as a model of light. In many ways this was helpful: it allowed scientists to understand various aspects of the behaviour of light on the assumption that light behaved just like sound. Now, sound requires a medium for its propagation—in other words, it needs to travel through something like air or water. An experiment I remember being shown at high school demonstrated how making a vacuum around a ringing bell stopped its sound travelling. The ringing bell was placed inside a large glass container, and the air was gradually pumped out. As this was being done, the sound of the bell became fainter and fainter until eventually we could no longer hear it. And so we realized that sound needed to travel through something.

It was therefore assumed that light also needed to travel through something, and the word 'aether' was coined to describe the medium through which light waves travelled. If you read old radio magazines, or listen to old radio programmes, you'll sometimes find people referring to 'waves travelling through the aether'. But by the end of the century it had become clear that light did not seem to need any medium to travel through. What had happened was simply that the logical necessity of one aspect of the model (sound) had initially been assumed to apply to what was being modelled (light), and this assumption was gradually recognized to be incorrect as the experimental evidence built up.

And so it is with models of God. For example, we often use 'father' as a very helpful model of God, emphasizing the way in which we are dependent upon God for our existence. But for every human child there is a human mother as well as a human father. This would seem to imply that there is a heavenly mother in addition to a heavenly father. But this assumption rests upon the improper transfer of the logical necessity of an aspect of the model (father) to what is being modelled (God), in just the same way as the necessity of one aspect (the need for a medium of propagation) of the model (sound) was transferred to what was being modelled (light). This is a difficult point, but well worth grasping, as it enables us to avoid making many of the mistakes which commonly arise through the biblical use of models to talk about God. Perhaps it is as well to ask ourselves what a given model, such as 'God as King', is *not* saying as much as what it *is* saying.

One final point needs to be made. In this chapter we have emphasized how the full complexity of the nature and character of God can be at least partially mediated through simple visual images, images which are often so simple that a child can understand them, just as scientific truths can often be mediated in the same way. Yet people very often seem unable to cope with this way of thinking about reality. You say to them, 'Why don't you think of an atom as a sort of golf ball?' and they respond, 'That's far too simple. I can't believe that. Surely you can give me something more sophisticated than that?' And so you try a different way of representing that atom. You take a piece of paper, write down a complicated mathematical function, and say, 'That's another way of representing an atom.' And they then respond, 'That's far too complicated. You're just blinding me with your science. Surely you can explain it in more simple terms than that?'

In many ways, this just goes to show that you can't please everyone all the time. But it also indicates the genuine difficulty that many—indeed, probably most—people have in understanding the way in which complicated things are described and portrayed. A golf ball and a wave function (the 'complicated mathematical expression' in the last paragraph) are both perfectly legitimate and proper ways of describing atoms, each with its own uses. And so it is with God. When we say that 'God is like a father—both severe and kind to his children', we very often get the response, 'I can't believe that. It's far too simple. I'm not a child aged six—give me something more sophisticated.' And so you talk about 'the need to recognize a creative dialectic between severity and kindness within the economy of salvation', only to be told, 'That's far too complicated. If there really is a God, I'm sure he would have made it more simple than all this abstract nonsense.' It's almost as if Christianity is something which was invented by human beings, and which stands or falls depending upon whether it is sophisticated in a simple way! But the reality of the situation is that we are trying to describe God as best we can at a number of levels. The little child can think of God as a loving shepherd, and the university professor as 'the ground of radical creativity'—but they are both thinking about the same God, only in different ways and at different levels.

One of the most exciting things about Christianity is that it allows God to be portrayed and conveyed in these very different ways, each of which allows genuine and helpful insights to be gained. The critic who won't believe Christianity either because it's too simple or because it's too complicated (depending upon which of these two objections you've just met) has probably already made his mind up about Christianity and doesn't want his prejudices disturbed. But for those for whom this is a genuine difficulty, the use of models in the world of science is an extremely helpful way of illustrating how simple pictures and models can mediate the most profound insights.

In the following chapter, we shall turn to look at the richness, vividness, immediacy and dramatic force of the biblical models of God in order to begin our discussion of God as a person.

4

Biblical Models of God

Let's suppose you're watching a drama on television. Perhaps it's a play, like *Arsenic and Old Lace* or *Romeo and Juliet*. The individual characters come onto the screen and you can see what they look like. You can also see the settings in which the action takes place. Your mental picture of the characters and the settings is given to you through the medium of television. Now imagine that you're listening to that same drama, except that it's being transmitted by a radio station. There is no picture to see, the only medium being presented to you is sound. You have to imagine what the characters look like; you have to imagine what the settings look like. Many people actually prefer the medium of radio because they find it more stimulating for this very reason.

In many ways, the biblical witness to God is very like a radio play. You are given a picture of God in words, not a series of photographs. You must sit down and think about God in terms of the verbal images which you are given, each of which is capable of giving several invaluable insights into God. And just as you have to try and wonder what the person behind the voice is really like, so we have to try and think what the reality behind these verbal images may be. Both the Old and New Testaments use models to stimulate and guide our thinking about God—verbal pictures of God which we can remember and reflect upon.

Before we examine some of these models, two points ought to be made. First, in the last chapter we pointed out how models were 'partial and conceivable representations of reality'. Does this not suggest that the Bible is giving us only a partial, and hence inadequate, picture of God? Certainly not! Scripture gives us a rich range of models which, like a child's toy bricks, build up to give a comprehensive and reliable picture of God. Each of these models, taken on its own, is certainly inadequate. God is a shepherd, for example—but there is a lot more that can and should be said about God than that. The biblical models of God are the building-blocks which combine to give a comprehensive picture of God.

Secondly, we need to note that we are authorized to use only certain models of God—those given in Scripture. As we have stressed, the primary source of our knowledge of God is Scripture. Indeed, we could say that God lays down the ways in which he wants us to think about himself. This means that we cannot just choose any old model and argue that it adequately represents God; we need to concentrate on those which we are given, and work out what it is that they are telling us about God. On the basis of these insights, we may well be able to come up with modern equivalents which mediate the same insights—for example, God as a probation officer, or a managing director. But we must remember that our attempts to devise contemporary models are always secondary to, and dependent upon, the scriptural testimony. The best preacher and communicator will be the person who, steeped in a knowledge of the biblical models of God, finds the most helpful contemporary analogies for them by reading the newspapers and watching television—but these are simply contemporary restatements of the original models. They do not have the same status as the God-given and authorized models which we find in Scripture. The preacher must therefore continually seek to relate the biblical models to the modern world, while never allowing the latter to supercede the former.

In the present chapter we're going to examine some of the biblical models of God in order to see how they combine to build up an overall portrayal of God. The biblical models for God are fresh and vivid, drawn from the everyday life of the period. These models include forces of nature, inanimate objects and human beings—all of which allow us to begin to think of God in a tangible manner. Although the passage of time has made some of these less vivid than they once were, it requires remarkably little effort to bring out their full force and vitality. We begin with one of the most familiar of all the biblical models of God.

1. God as shepherd

One of the most familiar verses in the Bible is Psalm 23:1—'The Lord is my shepherd.' This image of God as a shepherd is encountered frequently in the Old Testament (e.g., Psalm 80:1; Isaiah 40:11; Ezekiel 34:12), and is taken up in the New Testament to refer to Jesus, who is the 'good shepherd' (John 10:11). But what does this model tell us about God?

First, we encounter the idea of the loving care of the shepherd for his sheep. The shepherd was committed to his flock of sheep on a full-time basis. Indeed, the shepherd tended to be regarded as a social outcast in Israel on account of the enormous amount of time he was obliged to spend with his flock, which prevented him from taking part in normal social activities. The idea of God as a shepherd thus conveys the idea of the total commitment of God to his people. The idea is developed very powerfully in the New Testament, especially in the parable of the lost sheep (Luke 15:3-7). Here the shepherd actively seeks out the lost sheep in order to bring it home. The final intensification of the image is found in John's gospel, where it is emphasized that the good shepherd—who is immediately identified as Jesus—will willingly go so far as to lay down his life for the safety of his sheep (John 10:11-16).

Secondly, thinking of God as a shepherd speaks to us of guidance. The shepherd knows where food and water are to be found and guides his sheep to them. It is he who finds the green pastures and quiet waters (Psalm 23:2) for his sheep. I was brought up in the Irish countryside where flocks of sheep wander aimlessly around, giving every impression of being lost. Left to their own devices, sheep have a habit of getting lost and wandering off into dangerous countryside, becoming stranded on hillsides. It is the shepherd who keeps the sheep on safe ground and ensures that they have food and drink. To liken God to a shepherd is to emphasize his constant presence with his people, and his gentle guidance as he tries to protect them from the dangers of life and bring them to a place of plenty and safety. 'He tends his flock like a shepherd: he gathers the lambs in his arms and carries them close to his heart; he gently leads those that have young' (Isaiah 40:11).

Thirdly, the image of God as shepherd tells us something about ourselves. We are the sheep of God's pasture (Psalm 79:13; 95:7; 100:3). Like sheep, we are incapable of looking after ourselves and we continually go astray. We are not self-sufficient: just as the sheep rely upon the shepherd for their existence, so we have to learn to rely upon God. We may like to think that we are capable of looking after ourselves, but realism demands that we recognize just how totally dependent upon God we are from the moment of our birth to our death.

Human sinfulness is often compared with running away from God like a stray sheep: 'We all, like sheep, have gone astray, each of us has turned to his own way' (Isaiah 53:6; cf. Psalm 119:176; 1 Peter 2:25). Just as the shepherd goes to look for his lost sheep, so God came to find us in our lostness and bring us home. The parallels with the parable of the prodigal son (Luke 15:11-32) will be obvious. In fact, in Luke 15 we find three stories of 'lostness', all illustrating the idea of our being lost, then someone looking for us, and then rejoicing when they find us and bring us home. The shepherd finds his lost sheep (Luke 15:3-7); the woman finds her lost coin (Luke 15:8-10); the father finds his lost son (Luke 15:11-32). And in all these analogies we find the same constant emphasis of the gospel: we are lost but God has come into the world in his Son Jesus Christ in order to find us and bring us home rejoicing.

A final point which the model of God as shepherd makes with particular clarity concerns the nature of the relationship of the believer with God. The shepherd doesn't point his sheep in the right direction leading to the 'quiet waters and green pastures', but takes them there, carrying those who are too weak to make the journey unaided (Isaiah 40:11). Christianity is not about God telling us where to go and what to do if we want salvation, and then leaving us to get on with it—it is about God graciously accompanying, supporting and sustaining us as he journeys with us and guides us. Similarly, Jesus tells us that he is 'the way and the truth and the life' (John 14:6). He doesn't just show us the way that leads to eternal life, but sets us on that path and journeys with us as we travel. The great theme of 'Emmanuel'—God is with us (Matthew 1:23)—resounds throughout the Christian life as we remember that God is with us, even in life's darkest moments, guiding us to our eternal rest.

2. God as spirit

'God is spirit' (John 4:24). But what does this tell us about God? In dealing with this model we need to remember that the English language uses at least three words, 'wind', 'breath' and 'spirit', to translate a single Hebrew word, *ruach*. This important Hebrew word has a depth of meaning which it is virtually impossible to reproduce in English. This has the obvious result that if we want fully to understand the depths of meaning associated with the model of God as spirit, we need to try and understand the richness of this important model. Furthermore, we need to remember that by translating the Hebrew word *ruach* by 'spirit', many English versions of the Old Testament lose much of the richness of the original image. In the present section, we're going to try to unfold the richness of this very helpful way of thinking about God.

First, the idea of spirit is associated with life. When God created Adam, he breathed into him the breath of life, as a result of which he became a living being (Genesis 2:7). The basic difference between a living and a dead human being is that the former breathes and the latter doesn't. This led to the idea that life was dependent upon breath (and we recall that 'breath' is one of the senses of the Hebrew word *ruach*). God is the one who breathes the breath of life into empty shells and brings them to life. Just as God brought Adam to life by breathing into him, so God is able to bring individuals and his church to life through his Spirit today. The famous vision of the valley of the dry bones (Ezekiel 37:1-14) also illustrates this point: the bones only come to life when breath enters into them (Ezekiel 37:9-10). So the first idea that the model of God as spirit suggests is that God is the one who gives life, perhaps even the one who is able to bring the dead back to life.

The second idea that the model of God as spirit helps us understand is that of power. Here we are thinking especially of the wind (remembering that the Hebrew word *ruach* also has this meaning). All of us are used to seeing things being moved by an invisible force—the wind does it all the time. We often see papers blown across the road by the wind, or trees bending before its force. And in those areas of the world where hurricanes are common, entire towns may be destroyed by the power of this invisible force which we call the wind. The Old Testament writers, noticing the way in which the wind acted, could hardly fail to notice an obvious parallel with the way in which God acted. God is like the wind—an unseen force which acts upon things and people. I remember once being blown over by the wind while crossing a street, and feeling rather stupid about it afterwards!

We could develop this idea further. Let's suppose that you're starting a fire the hard way—by striking a spark onto some tinder which then begins to smoke. If you blow on the tinder, that little pile of smouldering tinder begins to glow and then catches fire, setting the whole pile of wood alight. So God breathes upon our faith in order to establish it and set us on fire with a love for himself. If you've been stupid enough to light that camp-fire in the middle of a forest while there's a strong wind blowing, the sparks from your fire could end up setting the whole forest ablaze. Yet it was only a little spark which started it off—with the help of the wind. In the same way, God is able to turn the spark of our faith into a burning fire which can set the world alight in much the same way as our camp-fire could set a forest alight. Thinking about God as the wind helps us understand how God is able to do so much with so little.

Wind is something which we know by its effects, rather than something which we know in itself. If we were pressed hard enough, we could probably give some sort of description of what the wind is—'air molecules in high-speed motion' perhaps. But we all find it much easier to speak about the wind in terms of what it does, rather than what it is. The wind is whatever it is that's blowing that piece of paper about. The wind is what's making that plume of smoke bend in that direction. The wind is the force that's blowing that enormous tree over. And so it is with God. Many people find it much easier to talk about God in terms of what he does, rather than in terms of what he is. God is whoever transformed my friend's life by bringing him to faith. God is whoever raised Jesus Christ from the dead.

We could develop this point a little further. Let's suppose that there have been high winds in your area recently, and as you walk around afterwards, when the wind has stopped blowing, you come across an enormous tree lying on the ground. It has been torn up from the ground with its roots still intact. How did it come to be there? It is almost certain that it has been blown down by the wind. We have got so used to seeing things being blown down by the wind, however, that we rarely reflect on how strange an event this is. How is it that infinitesimally small air molecules can knock an enormous tree down? After all, air is what we're breathing here and now, and it's not doing anybody any harm. We can't feel the wind any more, because it is calm. Yet the fallen tree stands as a witness to the presence and activity of the wind in the past. The fact that the wind is not blowing now does not mean that it didn't blow in the past and won't blow again in the future. The uprooted tree is a symbol of the unpredictability and power of the wind.

The parallels with the way in which God is present and at work within his world will be obvious. There may be moments when God seems to be present in our lives or in history in a powerful and exciting way, yet this may be followed by a period of calm, a period in which God does not give any indication of his presence. Like a sailing ship, we may find ourselves becalmed in the spiritual doldrums. Yet this may suddenly give way to renewed divine activity as the wind of God blows again in our lives and in history. The very unpredictability of the wind points to the fact that God acts in a way which we do not fully understand and cannot predict.

A third way in which the model of God as spirit is helpful concerns the various ways in which God's activity is experienced. Sometimes God is experienced as a judge, one who breaks us down in order to humble us; at other times he is experienced as one who refreshes us, like water in a dry land. The biblical writers were already familiar with the fact that one and the same thing could be experienced in different ways on account of their experience of the wind. To understand this, let us consider the two main types of wind known to the Old Testament writers.

Israel, we must remember, bordered the Mediterranean Sea on the west and the great deserts on the east. When the wind blew from the east, it was experienced as a mist of fine sand which scorched vegetation and parched the land. Travellers' accounts of these winds speak of their remarkable force and power. Even the light of the sun is obliterated by the sand-storm thrown up by the wind. This wind was seen by the biblical writers as a model for the way in which God demonstrated the finitude and transitoriness of his creation. 'The grass withers and the flowers fall, because the breath of the Lord blows on them' (Isaiah 40:7). Just as the scorching east wind, like the Arabian Sirocco, destroyed plants and grass, so God was understood to destroy human pride (see Psalm 103:15-18; Jeremiah 4:11ff.). Just as a plant springs up, fresh and green, only to be withered before the blast of the hot desert wind, so human empires rise only to fall before the face of God.

Thus, at the time when the prophet Isaiah was writing, Israel was held captive in Babylon. To many it seemed that the great Babylonian Empire was a permanent historical feature which nothing could change. Yet the transitoriness of human achievements when the 'breath of the Lord' blows upon them is asserted by the prophet as he proclaims the pending destruction of that empire. God alone is permanent, and all else is in a state of flux and change. 'The grass withers and the flowers fall, but the word of our God stands for ever' (Isaiah 40:8). The rise and fall of the Roman Empire, and more recently the British Empire, must remind us of this point, so powerfully developed through the model of God as the scorching desert wind.

The western winds, however, were totally different. In the winter, the west and south-west winds brought rain to the dry land as they blew in from the sea. In the summer, the western winds did not bring rain but coolness. The intensity of the desert heat was mitigated through these gentle cooling breezes. Just as this wind brought refreshment, by moistening the dry ground in winter and cooling the heat of the day in summer, so God was understood to refresh human spiritual needs. In a series of powerful images, God is compared by the Old Testament writers to the rain brought by the western wind (Hosea 6:3), refreshing the land. A friend of mine, who had spent some time working in East Africa, told me that one of the most remarkable sights he had seen was the effect of rain upon the dry land. What had been arid and barren ground suddenly turned green as all sorts of plant life seemed to appear from nowhere. In many ways this brings out the importance and meaning of the biblical model of God as the gentle west wind which brings rain to the thirsty land. We are like travellers through a dry land who suddenly discover an oasis. In the midst of our weariness and anxiety, God refreshes us.

3. God as parent

The image of a human parent is used to a considerable extent by both the Old and New Testament writers as a model of God. Although the strongly patriarchal structure of society at the time inevitably meant that emphasis was placed upon God as father (e.g., Jeremiah 3:19; Matthew 6:9), there are several passages which encourage us to think of God as our mother (e.g., Deuteronomy 32:18). We shall be considering these two images together, and ask what they tell us about God.

The first, and most obvious, point is that God is understood as the one who called us into being, who created us. Just as our human parents brought us into being, so God must be recognized as the author and source of our existence. Thus at one point in her history, Israel is chided because she 'forgot the God who gave [her] birth' (Deuteronomy 32:18; cf. Isaiah 44:2, 24; 49:15).

The second point which the model of God as parent makes is the natural love of God for his people. God doesn't love us because of our achievements, but simply because we are his children. 'The Lord did not set his affection on you and choose you because you were more numerous than other peoples, for you were the fewest of all peoples. But it was because the Lord loved you' (Deuteronomy 7:7-8). Just as a mother can never forget or turn against her child, so God will not forget or turn against his people (Isaiah 49:15). There is a natural bond of affection and sympathy between God and his children, simply because he has brought them into being. Thus God loved us long before we loved him (1 John 4:10, 19). Psalm 51:1 refers to God's 'great compassion', and it is interesting to note that the Hebrew word for 'compassion' (*rachmin*) is derived from the word for 'womb' (*rechmen*). God's compassion towards his people is that of a mother towards her child (cf. Isaiah 66:12-13). Compassion stems from the womb.

The Old Testament in particular often compares God's relationship with his people to a father's relationship with his young son. When the son is very young, he is totally dependent upon his father for everything, and their relationship is very close. But as the son grows older, he gradually comes to exercise his independence and break away from his father so that the relationship becomes more distant. The prophet Hosea uses this illustration to underline how Israel has become a virtual stranger to the God who called her into existence:

> When Israel was a child, I loved him, and out of Egypt I called my son. But the more I called Israel, the further they went away from me. They sacrificed to the Baals and they burned incense to images. It was I who taught Ephraim to walk, taking them by the arms; but they did not realise it was I who healed them. I led them with the cords of human kindness, with ties of love (Hosea 11:1-4).

This image is, of course, developed with enormous skill in the parable of the prodigal son (Luke 15:11-32). The point being made is that the natural love of the father for his son is wounded by the growing independence and alienation of the son. Like the prodigal son, we choose to go our own way, ignoring God. Yet the same God who created us also redeems us as he enters into human history in the person of Jesus Christ in order to find us, meet us, and bring us back to him. In many ways, the entire Bible can be read as the story of God's attempt to bring his creation back to him.

The third aspect of this model which is of interest concerns prayer. In the Sermon on the Mount, Jesus compares the believer's act of praying to God with a child's act of asking his father for something he wants (Matthew 7:7-11). The basic idea underlying this comparison is that even human fathers, despite being sinful, wish the best for their children. The child may ask for something outrageous, which the father refuses to give him, in the child's best interests. I can remember asking my father for a hunting knife when I was quite young. My father, being alarmed at what I might do with it, quite naturally refused—an action which I thought was quite unreasonable at the time. A few months later, a relative (knowing that I wanted such a knife) gave me one—and I promptly managed to cut myself very badly with it.

The parallels between the father and God, and the child and ourselves, are very clear. The child has a somewhat distorted and unrealistic view of what his own capabilities and

needs are, and his requests to his father reflect this immaturity. The father tries to help his child become more realistic
and mature by his responses to such requests. He may give the
child something which the child would never have thought of
asking for. But the fundamental assumption is that the relation of asking and giving between father and son is governed
by the father's love for his child, and his passionate desire for
the child's well-being. A similar relation exists between God
and the believer. Our requests to God all too often reflect our
immaturity and our unrealistic estimation of our needs. Like a
wise father, God tries to help us become more realistic and
mature by his responses to those requests. But his total love
for and dedication to us is not called into question by his
failure to meet all our requests.

4. God as light

'God is light' (1 John 1:5). The imagery of light and darkness
is often employed in both Old and New Testaments to help us
understand what God is like. But what does the model of God
as light tell us about him?

Let's begin with an image which occurs several times in the
Old Testament—that of watchmen waiting for the dawn (e.g.,
Psalm 130:6). The night was seen as a time of potential danger
when watchmen had to be posted throughout the city of Jerusalem in order to warn of any threat to the city which developed under the cover of darkness. The arrival of the dawn was
seen as marking the end of this threat—at least, for the time
being. Dawn thus came to be associated with hope, or with a
sense of relief. 'I wait for the Lord, my soul waits, and in his
word I put my hope. My soul waits for the Lord more than
watchmen wait for the morning' (Psalm 130:5-6). The ending
of the night was often seen as an image of the end of a period
of despair or misery, the dawning of a new period of life and
light, and particularly the dawning of the 'Day of the Lord',
the messianic era.

The rising of the sun marks that dawn, and it was natural
that the sun should be seen as an analogy of God (although it

must be remembered that the Old Testament always played this point down in case it led to sun-worship). Thus Malachi, the final prophetic work in the Old Testament, looks forward to a time when God will come to visit and redeem his people (Malachi 3:1-4; 4:1-2). The coming of God to his people is then compared to the rising of the sun: 'The sun of righteousness will rise with healing in its wings' (Malachi 4:2). This verse has been made famous through the Christmas carol 'Hark! the herald angels sing', even though the Hebrew is probably better translated as 'risen with healing in its *rays*':

> Hail, the heav'n-born Prince of Peace!
> Hail, the Sun of Righteousness!
> Light and life to all He brings,
> Ris'n with healing in His wings.

The same idea lies behind the famous messianic passage in Isaiah: 'The people walking in darkness have seen a great light' (Isaiah 9:2). The idea can, of course, be developed in other directions. For example, in an earlier chapter we saw how trying to get a direct glimpse of God was like staring into the sun—an impossibility, something which we simply are not capable of.

Secondly, light exposes things for what they really are. When I was a college student at Oxford, I was given a rather dilapidated room to live in during my second year. The walls were badly in need of painting, the carpet was worn through, and the windows were so dirty it was virtually impossible to see through them! In the daytime the room looked dreadful, but I soon discovered that you couldn't see any of this at night! By using subdued lighting, the room took on an almost magical quality. I couldn't see the dirty walls or windows, and the holes in the carpet were very difficult to spot unless you knew exactly where to look for them. It was the same room, but the absence of any strong light prevented all these things being noticeable. Of course, when daylight returned, I could hardly help noticing them again!

Light, then, shows things up—warts and all—for what they really are. When the shadows and half-lights are removed, we discover that they have been hiding the real state of things from our sight. In the light of the word of God (Psalm 119:105), we are shown up for what we really are—lost sinners, far from home, who need to return to God. The word of God is like a spotlight which picks us out and exposes us. It judges us simply by showing us up as we really are, scattering the shadows and darkness of our illusions of what we are like. In John's gospel we find Jesus being identified as the 'light of the world' (John 8:12; cf. 12:46). Jesus is the one who shows things up for what they really are, just as light does. 'If I had not come and spoken to them, they would not be guilty of sin. Now, however, they have no excuse for their sin' (John 15:22). In the light of Jesus, we realize how far short of God's standards we have fallen, and how much we need the grace of God if we are to be redeemed.

We can take the idea of Jesus as the 'light of the world' a little further. Let's suppose that you are in a small boat off a rocky coastline. As night falls, you realize that you cannot see the coast any longer, and are unsure how to navigate back to your home port. And then you see a light in the distance, flashing regularly—a lighthouse. While the Old and New Testament writers didn't know much about lighthouses, they had an equivalent—the city on the hill, lit up so that wayfarers could find their way to safety from the perils of the night (Matthew 5:14). Here we have the idea of a light showing us the way home. John's gospel in particular develops the idea of Jesus himself being the light which guides us home to God. Jesus is the 'light of the world' (John 8:12), just as he is 'the way and the truth and the life' (John 14:6) leading us to the Father.

This way of thinking about God also helps us understand how we, as Christians, are meant to be the 'light of the world' (Matthew 5:14). We all know what it is like to try and find our way out in the country at night, when there is no artificial light of any sort. It makes us realize how much we rely on the light of the sun. But not every night is dark. The light of the full moon, though much fainter than that of the sun, illuminates the night landscape and allows us to find our way. It may not show up every feature of the landscape—for that we have to wait for the sun. The moon is, in fact, simply reflecting the light of the sun—it has no light of its own. Taken by itself it is just a lifeless, barren, cold ball of moon-rock. Having no light, no source of power, of its own, it can still cast light on the earth by reflecting the brilliance of the sun.

So it is with us as Christians who, as 'the light of the world', reflect the glory of '*the* light of the world'. It isn't as if we possess some independent source of illumination—our light is based upon an external source which we reflect. Taking this a little further, we might recall that the moon shows phases—a process that used to be called 'waxing and waning'. The more of the moon that is illuminated, the greater the light it reflects to earth. The amount of light reflected depends upon the relative positioning of sun, earth and moon. And so it is with Christians—we must learn to place ourselves in the right position with both God and our fellow human beings if we are to be most effective witnesses.

5. God as a rock

The Old Testament frequently refers to God as a rock (e.g., Psalm 18:2; 28:1; 42:9; 78:35; 89:26; Isaiah 17:10). In many ways it may seem quite inappropriate to model God on an inanimate object such as a rock. However, the image is actually very helpful, conveying one simple and very powerful idea—security and reliability. Psalm 42:7, for example, develops a very vivid picture of the Psalmist being beaten down by a powerful flood, continually threatening to overwhelm and destroy him. And yet, in the midst of this sea of surging water, there is a place of security—the rock which is God (Psalm 42:9). A rock is something firm and immovable which can survive storms, floods and heat alike. It is a place of refuge. Thus Moses, when criticizing the Israelites for worshipping false gods, points to the close relation between God, rocks and safety: 'Where are their gods, the rock they took refuge in?' (Deuteronomy 32:37).

There is a story which is told about the eighteenth-century English hymn-writer Augustus Toplady. Once Toplady was out walking in the Malvern Hills, in south-western England, when a heavy rainstorm developed. Toplady is reported to have rushed to find shelter from the storm, eventually sheltering in a fissure in the rocky hills. As he sheltered in the rock from the storm, he began to reflect on the parallels between escaping from a rainstorm and escaping from the forces of sin, death and decay—and so he came to write his famous hymn:

> Rock of ages, cleft for me,
> Let me hide myself in Thee.

In thinking about God as a rock, we can think of him as a secure place of shelter from the storms of life, a place of refuge from sin and evil.

The famous hymn by John Newton makes this point well, and takes the imagery a little further:

> Dear name! the rock on which I build,
> My shield and hiding place.

Both the Old and New Testaments also encourage us to think of a rock as a secure foundation upon which we may build. This idea, of course, is developed most vividly in the Sermon on the Mount, with its famous parable of the house on the rock (Matthew 7:24-27). The basic idea being developed is that any construction, whether a house or an attitude to life, must rest upon a secure foundation if it is to survive. It cannot be built upon shifting sands, but must rest upon something permanent and enduring. In thinking of God as a rock, we are invited to reflect upon the fact that it is God, and God alone, who is unchanging and permanent, despite all the changes we see going on around us. It is on the rock of God alone that we must build our house of faith, knowing that only in this way can we weather the storms and floods of life.

The idea of God as a rock, then, conveys the important fact that God is something permanent and secure in a rapidly changing and unstable world: 'Who is God besides the Lord? And who is the Rock except our God?' (2 Samuel 22:32-33). God is our place of refuge, our hiding place, the firm foundation upon which we may base our lives and our faith. All these ideas are vividly captured by the model of God as a rock.

In this chapter we have looked at some of the biblical models of God in order to show how useful they can be. The everyday world gives us 'pegs' on which we can hang our thoughts about God, allowing us to avoid using highly abstract language about him. In many ways models are like parables, but whereas a parable is 'an earthly story with a heavenly meaning' (as every Sunday school student knows), a model is basically something drawn from everyday life which gives us insights into God. A parable is about a story, but a model is something from the world around us.

All of us know how difficult it can be to talk about God, and how hard it often is to find words which even begin to describe him adequately. In Scripture, however, we are given a way round this problem through a whole series of rich and powerful images which stimulate our imagination. For example, we are told by the biblical writers that God is like a rock, and immediately we begin to try and draw out the points of comparison. These simple, everyday images stimulate our thinking by forcing us to ask questions such as, 'In what way is God like a rock?' They are like discussion starters or conversation pieces—things which get us thinking and stop us being too abstract about God. They are pregnant with meaning and insights. It's very easy for Westerners, who are used to a conceptual way of thinking, to talk about God in hopelessly abstract ways. The biblical models of God bring us back to the concrete world of everyday things, and tell us that we can talk about God perfectly well without having to indulge in highly conceptual ways of thinking. Instead of talking about God as a 'creative and dynamic power' (a temptation to which theologians are prone), we can say that 'God is like the wind'—a much more vivid and creative way of talking, which immediately invites us (and anyone who happens to be listening) to start thinking about the ways in which God is like the wind.

In this chapter we've been looking at some of the biblical models of God, trying to draw out some of the insights they give us into what God is like, and the way in which he is present and active in his world. It may be that, as you read this chapter, you began to get some insights in addition to those here—if this happened, it just goes to prove how powerful and stimulating these models of God can be. Of course, we've only been able to look at a very limited number of models due to pressure on space. You might like to think about some additional models of God, not discussed here, and see what insights they give. Here are four you might like to try thinking about: God as king; God as friend; God as judge; God as fire.

In the following chapter we're going to look at what is often regarded as the most powerful of all biblical models of God—God as a person. What does it mean to talk about God as a person? What insights do we gain from talking about a 'personal God'? Are we justified in talking about a 'personal relationship with God'? It is to questions such as these that we now turn.

5

A Personal God

One of the most important Christian insights is that we are made in the image of God (Genesis 1:26-27). There is a basic likeness between ourselves and God which makes it possible for God both to present a picture of himself to us in human terms and to enter into a meaningful relationship with us. Both Old and New Testaments therefore draw extensively on language and ideas drawn from our own personal lives in order to help us understand what God is like. Personal language is the most helpful and reliable medium available for communicating the nature, character and purposes of God. Theologians often describe this way of thinking about God as *anthropomorphisms* (descriptions of God based upon human analogies, such as 'the arm of God' [Isaiah 51:9]) and *anthropopathisms* (descriptions of God based upon human emotions, such as 'the love of God').

For some, this way of thinking about God is very crude and primitive. It suggests to them that God is basically an old man in white robes enthroned on a cloud, which is far too unsophisticated an idea for the modern period. They would much rather think of God in more abstract terms, regarding him as a force or power behind the universe. Although this criticism may seem plausible initially, it actually rests upon a misunderstanding. The picture of an old man sitting on a cloud is simply a mental picture of what God is like, and not the reality of God. In an earlier chapter we pointed out that one of the simplest mistakes to make when using models, whether of God or of atoms, is to identify the model with what is being modelled. In other words, the image of an old man sitting on a cloud is just one way of thinking about God, just as the image of a golf ball is one way of thinking about atoms.

The basic point to realize is that anthropomorphic ways of thinking about God are concessions to our weakness. In other words, God knows how difficult it is for us to think about him, and so he gives us vivid learning aids in order to help us picture him in our minds. After all, we are always told that a picture is worth a thousand words! It is perfectly obvious from the biblical material that it is impossible to capture the rich-ness and profundity of God in human words. As a result, a whole range of pictures, models, images and metaphors have to be used, each of which casts light on one or two aspects of God's being and nature. None of them in itself is even re-motely adequate to do justice to who and what God is. As we saw in the last chapter, we can gain invaluable insights into God by thinking of him as a shepherd or as a rock—but that doesn't mean that God *is* a shepherd or a rock.

This point is so important that it deserves an illustration to bring it out. Let us take the biblical image of God as a rock and look at two ways of understanding it. The person who has completely missed the point of this way of thinking about God might say something like this: 'You are asking me to believe that God *is* a rock. I can't believe that. There are lots of rocks in my garden, but I don't worship them. How can you identify God with a lump of stone in this ridiculously unsophisticated way? I just can't believe in a God like that.' This person has made the elementary mistake of identifying the model (a rock) with what is being modelled (God). The person who understands the biblical ways of speaking about God would say something very different: 'So God is *like* a rock, is he? I suppose this means that in some way or other, a rock helps us understand what God is like. Now, when I think of a rock, I think of something that is permanent and secure, the sort of place you might build a castle on. And so God also represents a place of security and permanence, something on which I can build.' Do you see the crucial difference between these two ways of approaching the biblical ways of speaking about God?

One of the most remarkable things about the biblical way of speaking about God is that it is able to use the most unsophisticated starting-points to build up a remarkably sophisticated picture of God. Thus we could begin with the idea of a shepherd—something which is grounded in the everyday life of individuals, and which doesn't require any intellectual brilliance to grasp. Or we could begin from the idea of the wind, or our father or mother, or any of the many biblical models of God drawn from everyday experience. We then ask what these models tell us about God, and gradually build up an understanding of God. Although this understanding of God is based upon shepherds, rocks, the wind and so on, it completely transcends them.

We could take this idea a little further by thinking about an artist and his pictures, for example, Leonardo da Vinci and the *Mona Lisa*. As he paints, the artist applies colours to his canvas so that in one sense the resulting picture is nothing more than a mixture of colours. Yet the image which this mixture of colours conveys to us is the enigmatic face of the Mona Lisa. And it is this image that we see and which holds us spellbound. But behind this image stands a woman. We know virtually nothing about her. She is the reality behind the painting, the one who inspired the image which has intrigued generations of curious onlookers. Now, on the basis of this analogy, we have identified two different levels of representation of reality. First, we have a mixture of colours on a canvas. Secondly, we have the haunting image of the Mona Lisa which those colours combined to give. And thirdly, we have the Mona Lisa herself, the real creature of flesh and blood who is represented in that portrait. She is not identical with that portrait, but it corresponds to her, echoing her and capturing her likeness.

Those same three levels can be seen in the models of God

we use. First, they are collections of words—and how can human words adequately capture the greatness of God? Secondly, we have the image which those words combine to create in our minds: images of God as a shepherd, as a father, and so on. And thirdly, we have the reality of God himself. He is not identical with these verbal pictures, but they correspond to him, they echo him, and they capture his likeness.

Our response to the critic who dismisses God because he can't believe in an old man (or an enormous bearded nineteenth-century English clergyman!) sitting somewhere up in the clouds is therefore very simple. Everybody knows that the image of an old man sitting on a cloud is a totally inadequate representation of God, but this has no bearing on whether God exists or not, or what he is actually like. The same critic might refuse to believe in atoms because he finds it impossible to think of a world in which billions and billions of golf balls are flying around the place. He might refuse to believe that the Mona Lisa existed as a real person, because real persons are three-dimensional, not two, and move about, while the Mona Lisa has never altered her facial expression in centuries. But all he has actually done is drawn attention to the fact that both atoms and God—neither of which can be seen by the naked eye—are rather difficult to visualize without using models of some sort, and that the models used are sometimes not quite as good as we would like them to be. The question of the existence of God is quite independent of the difficulties we have in adequately understanding and visualizing him.

With these points in mind, let us begin to think about the idea of a personal God. What does it mean to speak of God as a person? The first point to make is that we are not saying that God is a human being. This point is obvious from our discussion of some of the models of God: when we say that God is our shepherd, we aren't saying that God is a human being surrounded by sheep, but what we are saying is that God is like a shepherd in various ways. In much the same way, we are saying that a human person is a good model for God. But in what way is God like a person?

The fundamental point behind the idea of a personal God is this: *God is able to enter into a personal relationship with us*. In other words, our relationship with other persons (our personal relationships) are analogous to our relationship with God. We don't relate to God in an abstract way, as if he was some diffuse cosmic force or moral principle, but in a personal way. We experience God in a personal manner, and our own personal relationships give us insights into our relationship with God. To give one very obvious example: when we talk about God as 'love', we are using a concept directly derived from the sphere of personal relationships. This fact is acutely embarrassing for some theologians, who want to abandon belief in a personal God on the basis of their questionable belief that the modern world can't cope with it. Thus John Robinson, in his once-famous book *Honest to God*, declares that our image of a personal God must go—and yet insists that our most profound experience is of God as love!

What insights, then, does the idea of a personal God allow us to gain? How is our understanding of the nature and character of God illuminated by human personal relationships? Space allows us to consider only a few.

The first insight is well known, and requires little discussion. We have already seen how there is a world of difference between *knowing about* a person and *knowing* a person. To know about someone or something is simply to produce a list of facts we know about them—the colour of their hair, their height, their weight, their family history, and so on. To know someone, on the other hand, is to experience them in a personal manner. It is to enter into a relationship with them in which they know us and we know them. It is a mutual, shared experience. The concept of *reciprocity* is central here: a personal relationship involves A knowing B, and B knowing A, whereas it is quite possible for A to know an enormous amount *about* B without B even knowing that A exists. For example, I know something about the present President of the United States, but that doesn't mean that he knows the first thing about me. The Christian understanding of our relationship with God is that this is a mutual relationship—it is not just a matter of us knowing something *about* God, but of us *knowing* God and *being known by* God.

Secondly, personal relationships establish the framework within which words such as 'love', 'trust' and 'faithfulness' have their meaning. Both the Old and New Testaments are full of statements concerning the 'love of God', the 'trustworthiness of God', and the 'faithfulness of God'. 'Love' is a word which is used of personal relationships. Furthermore, the great biblical theme of promise and fulfilment is based ultimately upon a personal relationship, in that God promises certain definite things, such as eternal life and forgiveness, to certain individuals. One of the great themes which dominates the Old Testament in particular is that of the covenant between God and his people, by which they mutually bind themselves to each other: 'I will be their God, and they will be my people' (Jeremiah 31:33). The basic idea underlying this is that of the personal commitment of God to his people, and of his people to their God.

This context of a personal relationship between God and his people also allows us to make sense of some biblical ideas which otherwise might seem rather strange. For example, we often find reference to God being jealous (Numbers 25:11; Deuteronomy 4:24; 32:16; 1 Kings 14:22; Psalm 78:58; 79:5; Ezekiel 8:3-5; Zechariah 1:14). Does it not seem rather strange to think of a good God being jealous? However, when we consider the background to this term, its meaning and relevance become obvious. God is the one who loves his people. He is the one who brought them into being, delivering them from Egypt and leading them into the promised land (Hosea 11:1-4). He loves his people so much that he is prepared to give his only Son up for them (John 3:16). Just as a husband and wife swear that they will love and stand by each other no matter what the future holds, so God and his people declare in the covenant that they will be faithful to each other. God is totally committed to the safety and well-being of his people. And it is clear that this love relationship is precious to God, that it means everything to him.

Imagine that you have fallen in love with someone, and

have done everything you can to further their well-being and safety, even to the point of risking your own career or life. And this person, in turn, falls in love with you, and a permanent relationship results. You swear eternal love to each other. How many romantic novels have been written on this very theme. But then someone else comes along and seduces this person who means everything to you. Your relationship seems to be in ruins. How would you feel about it? Again, countless romantic novels have been written on this theme as well. One of the Old Testament books, Hosea, explores this theme with great skill and compassion.

Hosea draws a parallel between the situation of a man and his faithless wife and that of God and Israel. Although God loved Israel passionately and totally, the fact remained that Israel preferred to follow other gods in his place. God said, 'I am the Lord your God, who brought you out of Egypt. . . . I cared for you in the desert, in the land of burning heat. When I fed them, they were satisfied; when they were satisfied, they became proud; then they forgot me' (Hosea 13:4-6). The work ends by portraying God musing over the delight he will experience when he welcomes his wayward people home (Hosea 14:4-7).

It is within this context that we are to understand the jealousy of God. It is no bitter, wounded pride, but the result of total mutual dedication and commitment being shattered through the infidelity of one party, while the other party remains totally committed and dedicated. As Scripture continually emphasizes, God's faithfulness is not cancelled by our faithlessness. Two illustrations, both drawn from the world of personal relationships, are used to make this point. First, there is the rupture of the relationship between husband and wife through adultery. Secondly, there is the alienation of a son from his father, so powerfully described in the parable of the prodigal son. Both can be restored through repentance and forgiveness. To speak of the jealousy of God is not to imply that his pride is wounded through our infidelity, but simply to emphasize the full extent of his love and commitment to us. God made us for himself in order that both might enjoy the resulting relationship, and he is grieved, both for himself and for us, through our lack of faithfulness to him. God's jealousy is an expression of his love for and commitment to us, his burning desire that we shall be his and he shall be ours.

The personal framework which establishes the meaning of the word 'love' is of importance in another context—one which is all too often overlooked. The doctrine of universalism is taken seriously in several of the more rationalist sections of the Christian church, largely because it is held to be inconceivable that a God of love should not wish to save everyone. It is argued that God will save everyone on account of his loving character—but this is so obviously wrong. The doctrine of universalism is actually a denial of God's love. To see why this is so, let us look at the question more closely. Love is about the reciprocal free response of two individuals. A loves B freely, and B loves A freely. To talk about being forced to love someone is something of a contradiction in terms. How many romantic novels have been written with the following basic plot: A loves B, but B loves C, and C loves B. A discovers that the father of B has committed some dreadful secret sin, and threatens to expose and ruin him unless B marries him. So B marries A—but she still loves only C.

The problem about universalism is that it requires that everyone—whether they like it or not—is forced to love God and be loved by him in return. A fundamental and God-given human freedom is completely compromised. The essence of the gospel is that God proclaims and demonstrates his love for us by sending his Son Jesus Christ to die for us, but does not force us to respond to him. We are given the enormous privilege of saying no to God if we do not wish to return that love. Faith is basically saying yes to the love of God, allowing a love relationship to develop. In no way does God force us to respond positively to him.

Now, let us suppose that an individual decides that he simply does not want to love God or be loved by him: he wants to say no to God. Universalism, however, declares that he *must* be saved: even though he does not *want* to be saved, he *must* be. His personal freedom and rights, given by God, are to be violated in the name of a dogma. Universalism declares that what this person wants is of no consequence: he *must* be saved. The most dreadful and distressing image results—one of God forcing this individual to abandon his own wishes, demanding that he respond to him, and refusing to take no for an answer. This is a sub-Christian view of God. The Christian view is of a God who offers his love to individuals in order that they may respond; the universalist view is of a God who forces his love upon individuals, irrespective of their integrity and wishes. God's love is something offered, not something imposed. To put it in a manner which some may find offensive, but which corresponds exactly to what is being said: Christianity speaks of God *loving* us, but universalism speaks of God *raping* us. Neither Scripture nor the Christian tradition knows anything of so repulsive a doctrine, which it has rightly and consistently rejected as sub-Christian and unworthy of the God whom we know and meet in Jesus Christ.

Thirdly, thinking of God as a person helps us understand the powerful appeal which Christianity has always had, and enables us to avoid blunting its force through misrepresenting or misunderstanding it. Christianity is not about a set of interesting ideas but about a person. If it were about a set of interesting ideas, we would find ourselves confronted with a number of serious difficulties. Christianity would appeal primarily to those who regarded themselves as intellectuals, who were able to handle ideas. Christianity would be perverted into a form of intellectual élitism which most of humanity is disqualified from grasping. And ideas, as anyone who has worked in the field of history knows, have a habit of going out of fashion, often never to make a come-back. It would be remarkable if some ideas originating in first-century Palestine were found to be of continuing relevance in the modern world, which faces a completely different cultural, social and intellectual situation. And anyway, having an interesting idea may be exciting at the time, but the excitement soon wears off. I can remember my excitement at first encountering some interesting ideas as a student, including the Quantum Theory, but once the novelty of the ideas wore off, I found myself getting bored by them. It's like reading a very short book: the first time round, it's quite interesting, but each time you read it, it gets less and less interesting until eventually it gets boring. We need more than interesting ideas about God to keep us going for the rest of our lives.

Thinking of God as a person immediately overcomes this difficulty. Suppose that you meet someone at a party—let's call this individual John Smith. After talking to him for a while, you learn the following things about him: he is male, aged twenty-five, likes French cookery, went to Switzerland on holiday last year, and plays the piano. Next time you meet him, you might learn more about him. But what is also happening is that you are getting to know—not just know about—John Smith. You begin to relate to him as a person, as John Smith, and not just the individual who is male, aged twenty-five, who likes French cooking, went to Switzerland last year, and plays the piano. You discover you like him, and a relationship begins to develop between you in which *facts about* John Smith increasingly become less important, and *John Smith himself* becomes increasingly important. All of us know about this from experience.

Let's take this a little bit further. As you get to know and like John Smith better, you find that he comes to exercise an increasing influence over you. You start to take his ideas seriously, and so on. Of course, this process may well be mutual, in that you will influence John Smith as well. We change through the influence of other people—they affect us. In other words, personal relationships are *transformational*: we are changed through the influence of other people. And so it is with God. Knowing God and having a relationship with God means being changed by God. Many of us know by personal experience that our lives are changed when we meet God. We try to become better people, to become more like God himself.

Another point that ought to be made concerns preaching. Let's suppose that you are convinced that a friend of yours would benefit greatly from getting to know John Smith. You try to persuade them of this fact. How would you do it? You could say something like this: John Smith is male, aged twenty-five, likes French cooking, went to Switzerland for a vacation, and plays the piano. In other words, you're just telling them facts about him. You are helping your friend to *know about* John Smith. But what you really want to do is not to tell them about John Smith, but to set up a situation in which they can meet and encounter each other, in which your friend can get to *know* him. You want to point him in the direction of John Smith, and suggest that he can and should meet him. You could tell him that John Smith is to be found at such-and-such a place, and that he's a really nice person.

Much the same applies to preaching about God. We could tell someone a lot about God, perhaps even giving him several textbooks to read, but what we really want to do is to point him in the right direction, and allow him to discover God for himself. In effect, what we are saying is: this is how *I* came to meet God, and I can assure you I am profoundly grateful that I did. Why don't you try to meet God in the same way, and see what happens? Preaching the gospel is basically pointing away from ourselves to the person who lies behind our faith, and proclaiming that this person makes himself available for those who seek him. The preacher is like a signpost, pointing towards God and declaring that he's a lot nearer than we might think.

In John's gospel we read of how Philip tells Nathanael about Jesus, declaring that the long-awaited Messiah has finally come: 'We have found the one Moses wrote about in the Law, and about whom the prophets also wrote—Jesus of Nazareth' (John 1:45). Nathanael argues that this is impossible—how can the Messiah come from Nazareth of all places? Philip, however, avoids the trap that all too many preachers fall into—getting stuck in dead-end arguments. Instead of launching into a long and rather pointless speech about the origins of the Messiah, he simply says, 'Come and see' (John 1:46), And Nathanael goes and looks—and is convinced by who and what he finds: 'Rabbi, you are the Son of God; you

are the King of Israel' (John 1:49). In many ways this illustrates perfectly the chief function of any preacher: to an-
nounce that God is near at hand, and then invite his hearers to
'come and see', allowing God to take over the situation from
that point onwards. His hearers encounter a living person, not
a lifeless and abstract idea. When we suggest that our friends
meet John Smith, our job is simply to point them in the right
direction—John Smith may be relied upon to do the rest,
simply because of who and what John Smith is. Likewise, our
preaching is primarily concerned with setting up the conditions under which our audience may encounter God—by
proclaiming their need for God and pointing them in the right
direction in order that they may encounter him.

Another point which ought to be made concerns the way in
which we experience people. When someone important dies,
there are usually lots of TV interviews with people who knew
him. And one of the most interesting things that usually
emerges from these interviews is that these people all knew
the dead person from different angles, seeing him in a different light. Sometimes it's difficult to believe that they're all
talking about the same person! However, it was the same
person they knew, in every case—they just knew and experienced him in different ways. There is something very personal
about each of their recollections, reflecting the simple fact
that the dead person related to each of them individually, in
different ways. They may all have known roughly the same
things *about* this dead person—when he was born, who his
family were, what his achievements were, how he died, and so
on. But they still *knew* him in different ways.

It will be obvious that we encounter a similar situation with
God. We may all know roughly the same things *about* him,
but we all *know* him in different ways, for he relates to us as
individuals, just as any other person. God isn't like some sort
of inanimate object, such as a block of wood, which is passive
and static—he is active and dynamic, relating to each and
every one of us in different ways. This point is probably easy
enough to understand, but it does have a very important result
which we all too often overlook.

When we talk about God, we are partly talking about *the way in which we know God*. And the way in which each of us knows God is rather personal. The way I know God and experience him is probably rather different from the way you know and experience him. Now, suppose I was trying to persuade someone that it would be a good idea for him to come to know God. I would probably explain to him the way in which I knew and experienced God, and imply that he could know and experience God in the same way. But God might relate to this individual in a totally different way. I might even put this person off wanting to know God, simply because of what attracted me personally to God. This individual might be attracted to God for reasons which are very different from my own. It is for reasons such as these that preaching must be recognized as pointing *away* from the faith of the individual believer and *towards* the basis and content of that faith—the living God himself.

A further point concerns the way in which we know other persons—a way which distinguishes them from objects. This point has been discussed considerably during the present century, particularly by philosophers such as Martin Buber. We shall introduce this point by considering an analogy. Let's contrast the way we know another person from the way in which we know a table or a chair. The table or chair remains static as we investigate it: it is passive, and we are active. We can treat it as an object, and we always retain the initiative in studying it. What we know about it can be expressed in terms of statements such as 'the weight of this table is such-and-such', or 'the dimensions of this chair are such-and-such'.

But when we come to study another person, we find that a very different situation develops. The other person is active, not passive. Although we may start to try and find out about them, the situation can be reversed very quickly: the other person can take the initiative away from us by starting to question us before we have a chance to question them. Interviewing people can be very easy, provided they let you ask all the questions and just confine themselves to answering. In this way you can find out about them without letting them find out very much about you. But sometimes the person who is being interviewed turns the tables and starts questioning his interviewers. And unless the interviewers regain the initiative very quickly, the situation can become chaotic. Persons are active subjects, not passive objects. Martin Buber thus distinguishes between *experience* (in which we are dealing with a passive object like a table) and *encounter* (in which we are dealing with an active subject, such as another person). We experience a chair, but we encounter a person.

When we try to describe our knowledge of a person, we find it difficult to do in exactly the same way as we might with a table. We can give their weight and dimensions in each case, and give a good physical description of what they look like. But there is something about a person which we cannot describe—we cannot just reduce them to a set of statistics or a system of descriptive terms. Imagine someone very close to you who means a lot to you. Now think of all the things you know about them—their age, their weight, their height, the colour of their eyes, and so on. Perhaps you could make a list on a piece of paper. But when you have finished—no matter how long that list is—you will soon realize that you haven't been able to describe that person properly. You could give that list to someone else and ask them if they feel that they *know* that person on the basis of what you've said about them. The answer will be no—they may now know a lot *about* this person, but they won't *know* them. Why not? Partly because you just cannot describe something so complex as a person in this way. But also partly because knowing is a *two-way process*, in which we are known by someone else as much as knowing someone else. If A knows B, then B knows A. It is this important insight which Buber tried to get across with his idea of 'encounter', which points to a mutual meeting of two persons.

The relevance of these insights to our discussion of God as a person will be obvious. First, we can't treat God as an object, something which we can examine at our leisure and under conditions of our choosing. Many nineteenth-century theologians in particular seemed to treat God as some sort of biological specimen, held captive in a cage, which they could examine in any way they pleased. This view of God fell out of fashion after the First World War, with the growing realization that God must be recognized as God, and cannot be treated in this demeaning way. He is someone active, someone who takes the initiative away from us and seeks us before we seek him. The Bible emphasizes the initiative of God in seeking us, and has little time for any idea of religion as our seeking after God. We are placed in the position of responding to God. It might well be that we would like to be in the position of interviewers who can ask God all the questions, keeping him under our control—but unfortunately it is God who is conducting the interview, under conditions which he has chosen. We have lost the initiative to God, and must learn to respond to him as he has disclosed himself.

It will also be clear that Buber's philosophy (sometimes referred to as 'dialogical personalism'), with its idea of an encounter between God and man modelled on an encounter between two human persons, lends added weight to the crucial distinction between *knowing about* God and *knowing* God—a distinction which we have already drawn attention to in this book. Any understanding of God which forbids us to speak of *knowing* God condemns itself as inadequate and inauthentic, and is simply sub-Christian. Christian prayer, for example, with its emphasis upon petition (that is, asking God for things), is modelled on the relation between two human persons, as we have seen (note especially Matthew 7:7-11). If an understanding of God is not capable of explaining why Christians pray to God in this way, it is once more to be rejected as simply incapable of bearing the crucial insights of the Christian faith. It may seem to make more sense to some modern souls to speak of God as 'the ground of our being', 'ultimate reality', or some similar abstract way of speaking, but it doesn't make much sense of the practice of Christian prayer. And how can we *know* 'ultimate reality' anyway? Isn't it really something (note the deliberate use of the word 'thing'!) which we can at best *know about*?

Thinking about God as a person, then, illuminates and safeguards many essential Christian insights about the nature and character of God. The supreme illustration of God as a person, however, is to be found in the incarnation. In Jesus Christ we encounter none other than God in the embodiment of a human person. In the following chapter we shall explore how the recognition that Jesus Christ is none other than the living God himself both confirms and develops the idea of God as a person, and lays the foundation for the distinctively Christian insights into God safeguarded by that most enigmatic of Christian doctrines—the doctrine of the Trinity. Curiously, it is through recognizing the full implications of affirming that God is a person that we are set on the road which leads to the recognition that God is *three* persons.

6

The Incarnate God—Jesus Christ

In an earlier chapter I asked you to imagine that you had lived in a dungeon all your life, with no knowledge of the outside world at all. And then someone who knew that world arrived and began to draw sketches of it. Although your knowledge of that outside world would be fragmentary and a little confused, you would at the very least become aware that there was something beyond the walls which held you captive. Now imagine that you are in that situation—in a dungeon, *knowing* that there was something beyond those walls, and excited by rumours and hints of what it was like. For a long time, you wonder what it is like, perhaps lying awake at night and imagining what you might be able to see one day.

And then you hear something. There is a noise coming from one of the walls, about halfway up. It starts off as a gentle scraping, and you have to listen carefully to work out whether your ears are playing tricks on you or not. Then it becomes louder, and you know that something is happening. Then suddenly a hole the size of your hand appears in the wall, and you realize that someone has drilled through the wall. As the dust subsides, a brilliant beam of light dazzles your eyes. You have lived in darkness for so long that your eyes have become accustomed to the gloom, and they have to readjust to the new situation. Then, anxiously, you creep up to the hole and look through it. And there, beyond the thick stone wall, you catch a glimpse of the world outside—a world of light and colour, of motion and sound. The hole isn't large enough to allow you to see everything, and the sound is distorted by the echo of the hole in the wall. But you have suddenly been presented with a new, direct vision of the world beyond.

You had been prepared for what you now see by the drawings you had once been shown, but now you realize for the first time the full significance of those two-dimensional static sketches. You see a tree, gently swaying in the breeze, gloriously green against a blue sky, and you realize that this is what the static two-dimensional monochrome sketch represented. Perhaps the subtle fragrance of fresh air, charged with the perfume of the flowers, begins to permeate and refresh the stale atmosphere of your prison. And suddenly a new perspective on your situation begins to dawn as you realize that there is an exciting new world outside, beckoning to you, calling you, inviting you to participate in it. It is *there* and you are *here*—but somehow it seems much nearer at hand than you could ever have imagined.

The parallel between this analogy and the Christian understanding of the incarnation is clear. 'In the past God spoke to our forefathers through the prophets at many times and in various ways, but in these last days he has spoken to us by his Son [who] . . . is the radiance of God's glory and the exact representation of his being' (Hebrews 1:1-3). In the Old Testament prophets, law and writings, we learn of God's gradual revelation of himself to his people. Like people trapped in a dungeon, they gradually realized that there was more to reality than what they could see—that the bounds of time and space did not exhaust a description of reality. Initially, they learned 'in various ways' of what God is like, through the verbal pictures they were given by the prophets. Each stage of this revelation laid the foundation for the next, until finally the scene was set for the great breakthrough. This was not a breakthrough which men made from their side of the walls of time and space, but one which God made from his side. The Old Testament prepared the way for this break-through, giving us inklings of what the world on the other side was like, and encouraging us to await and listen for the sound of the tunnelling.

And then, when the breakthrough came, the verbal pictures of God we had been given were seen in their true light. We were able to understand, perhaps for the first time, what they really meant. Those hints of the coming of the suffering servant (Isaiah 53), those rumours of the vindication of the righteous sufferer (Psalm 22), those promises that the Lord would suddenly come to his temple (Malachi 3:1)—all are suddenly seen in a new light as the reality to which they bear witness is seen for the first time. No longer are we dependent upon descriptions of what God is like, passed down from one generation to another—God himself 'has come and has redeemed his people' (Luke 1:68). God himself comes to us, in the form of a person—Jesus Christ. Setting aside his glory, power and majesty, God humbled himself and stooped down in order to meet us where we are, in a form with which we could identify. Jesus reflects, echoes and embodies what God is like—in short, Jesus is God in the flesh, God incarnate.

Our imaginary prisoners in that dungeon might pick up their two-dimensional monochrome picture of a tree, and compare it with the three-dimensional coloured image which they saw through the hole in the wall, and suddenly declare, 'So *that's* what this was all about! Now we can see that these pencil strokes here represent those branches, and these the leaves, but before we weren't quite sure exactly what they were meant to represent.' What had been slightly unclear before, perhaps even enigmatic, is suddenly recognized for what it really represents. And so it is for the Christian reading the Old Testament in the light of the coming of God in Jesus Christ. The Old Testament law and prophets are illuminated, are seen in a new light, because what they are representing and pointing to is suddenly made available. Thus Matthew takes a certain delight in taking his reader through a gamut of Old Testament prophecies (e.g., Matthew 1:22-23; 2:5-6, 15, 17-18, 23; 3:3), effectively saying, 'Now we know what these prophecies are really all about.'

Through Jesus Christ, whom we recognize to be God incarnate, a direct and personal encounter between ourselves and God is made possible. The one who the great Old Testament figures knew indirectly and incompletely takes the initiative and comes to us as one of us. One of the most powerful passages dealing with the relation between the faith of the great Old Testament heroes and those of the Christian era in the New Testament is Hebrews 11:1-12:2. In this great passage the writer points out how the Old Testament figures knew what the promises of God were leading up to, even though they themselves did not live to see it happen. All these people were still living by faith when they died. They did not receive the things promised; they only saw them and welcomed them from a distance' (Hebrews 11:13; cf. 11:39-40). The same theme can be seen in Luke's account of the encounter between the infant Jesus and Simeon (Luke 2:25-35). Here Luke rather tenderly allows us to witness the reaction of an old man who realizes that the moment he and countless others had waited for expectantly—the coming of God to his people—had finally happened (Luke 2:29-32).

Why do Christians believe that Jesus *is* God? (For a discussion of this point, see *Understanding Jesus*, pp. 63-119.) It must be emphasized that this was not an eccentric conclusion reached by some single misguided early Christian thinker, rather it represented the considered judgement of the whole Christian community as it reflected on the evidence they either knew at first hand—the life, and supremely the death and resurrection of Jesus Christ—or the witness to this evidence contained in the New Testament documents. In the long period of debate in the early church over this matter, no other explanation of the identity and significance of Jesus Christ was found to be adequate to do justice to the Christian experience of God through Jesus Christ, or the New Testament evidence itself. This was the collective conclusion of the Christian community over a period of centuries, not the unilateral decision of an autocratic and eccentric theologian! In Jesus Christ we encounter none other than the living God. If

Jesus Christ was just a human being, then he is no more relevant to our thinking about God than any other human being who has put his mind to the question down the ages. But on the other hand, the church was equally insistent that if Jesus Christ was to be identified with God in a simplistic manner, so that his humanity was denied or neglected, he would be entirely irrelevant to human life. The danger of thinking of Jesus as God, and God alone, however, only arose once the fact that he *was* God in the first place had become generally established.

In the modern period, of course, we have seen a number of challenges to the idea that Jesus is none other than God incarnate. One of the most frequently heard complaints concerning the doctrine of the incarnation is that it is illogical. Some recent theologians have asserted that to say that Jesus is God is just as logically inconsistent as saying that a circle is a square. Being human excludes being divine. But is this really right? Let's look at this carefully.

Circles and squares belong to the world of shapes, and are mutually exclusive—in other words, being a circle means *not* being a square, a triangle, or any other shape. The common logical world that both squares and circles occupy is that of *shapes*. To say that something is 'both a circle and a square' is first of all to say that this 'something' is a *shape*. When we go on to ask what sort of shape it is, we find a logical contradiction involved: we are told that it is two different and mutually incompatible shapes at one and the same time. And so a logical contradiction results. A similar situation arises within the world of colours. Red and blue occupy mutually exclusive territories in the common world of colours—a colour may be red or blue or something else, but not both red and blue. Once more, a simple logical contradiction results if we say that such and such a colour is red and blue at one and the same time.

But what is the common logical world occupied by God and man? Why are God and man logically incompatible? A circle and a square are two different shapes; red and blue are two different colours; God and man are two different—well, two different *what*? The simple fact is that they are just *different*, and not in any way logically incompatible. Let's go back to our colours and shapes. Something cannot be both a circle and a square, but something can be a *red square*. There is nothing logically inconsistent about something being both red and a square—the two ideas are drawn from different logical worlds. 'Red' and 'square' are different ideas, to be sure, but the idea of something which is both red and square certainly involves no contradiction. Similarly, 'God' and 'man' are drawn from different logical worlds—and thus in asserting that Jesus is both God and man, no logical contradiction of any sort is involved.

A more sophisticated analysis of the question of the logical relationship of 'God' and 'man' in the incarnation is due to perhaps the greatest of all English theologians, William of Ockham. In the fourteenth-century Ockham demonstrated, with considerable logical rigour, that no inconsistency of any kind was involved in the concept of the incarnation—and then went on to demonstrate how this helped us better understand the nature of the incarnation. But the basic point we are emphasizing is obvious: the assertion that the idea of Jesus being divine is absurd because it involves 'logical contradiction' is not to be taken too seriously.

We are also told by some modern theologians that the doctrine of the incarnation is irrelevant to the modern situation, and that everything that needs to be said about Jesus can be said, and said well, without the need to involve the idea of the incarnation. In fact, however, this is not the case. Let's look at some examples to bring this point out.

First of all, let's ask why we are talking about Jesus Christ at all. Why is he so special? Why has Christianity singled out this person, and this person alone, as supreme among human beings? The traditional answer has always been that the resurrection from the dead demonstrates that Jesus Christ is divine, and thus establishes that he has a unique status and identity which distinguishes him from all other human beings. There may well have been other human beings whose conduct and personality distinguished them—people such as Socrates in the ancient world, or Gandhi in more recent history—but we rightly respect these people as fellow human beings, not as God incarnate. Jesus' uniqueness is, for the Christian, ultimately grounded in *who he was,* rather than *what he said and did.* In other words, Christians have always tended to regard Jesus' teaching and lifestyle as of importance because of who they knew him to be, rather than because of what this teaching and lifestyle were in themselves.

Let's suppose that we eliminate the idea of Jesus being God incarnate, as some modern thinkers suggest we can. How, then, are we to justify the unique position which Jesus has always possessed for Christians? The answer, simply stated, is that it cannot be justified. What conceivable relevance can the teachings of a first-century Palestinian male have for us today, in such a totally different cultural setting? There is an enormous gulf separating first-century Palestine from the twentieth-century West, and anyone who has failed to realize this has probably not even begun to wrestle with the enormity of the problem. For example, many feminists argue that Jesus' teaching is compromised by his very masculinity, as well as the patriarchalism of his social context. So why should we pay any attention to Jesus? How can we justify his uniqueness with reference to his teaching? The answer seems to be that we cannot, unless we recognize that Jesus *was* someone very different from the rest of us, and that this point of difference is of central importance.

For traditional Christianity, the incarnation demonstrates that God has come among us as one of us, addressing us and calling us personally. It does not matter greatly *when* this happened in history—the important point is that it *did* happen, and that it thus tells us something important about who God is and what he is like. But if the idea of the incarnation is abandoned, we are left with the picture of a Jewish rabbi, distant in time, whose teaching and lifestyle may have singled him out in his own day, but who has little relevance in ours. It becomes difficult, to say the least (and many would simply acknowledge that it is utterly impossible), to justify the unique position which Jesus has always had for Christians. Far from being the centre of the Christian faith, he becomes relegated to the margins.

For, as even many critics of the incarnation are prepared to admit, Christians simply do not relate to Jesus as a distant figure from the past, but as the present and living Lord. They do not regard him as a distant teacher from the past, a long-dead rabbi or guru—they know him as their risen Lord, one whom they worship and through whom they know the living God. The doctrine of the incarnation preserves these central insights, without which Jesus sinks into near-oblivion as the historical founder of a religion which now seems content to do without him. To abandon faith in the incarnation is to lose sight altogether of the centrality of Jesus to the Christian faith.

A second point which may be made concerns the rise of a particular form of atheism in the twentieth century. This movement is sometimes known as 'protest atheism', on account of the fact that it 'protests' against a certain concept of God. The twentieth century has witnessed human cruelty and ferocity rarely paralleled in the history of the world. The horrors of the First World War in Europe, of the Stalinist purges in the Soviet Union, of the Nazi extermination camps, and of the programmes of genocide in South-East Asia—all have raised the question in the minds of many people concerning how God is involved in this world of suffering. Protest atheism is directed against the image of a God who stands aloof from his world while such suffering continues. To abandon the incarnation is to abandon the crucial Christian insight that God in Christ subjected himself to the cruelty and evil of the world.

A playlet entitled *The Long Silence* brings out this insight with remarkable force.

The Long Silence

At the end of time, billions of people were scattered on a great plain before God's throne. Most shrank back from the brilliant light before them. But some groups near the front talked heatedly —not with cringing shame, but with belligerence.

'Can God judge us? How can he know about suffering?' snapped a pert young brunette. She ripped open a sleeve to reveal a tattooed number from a Nazi concentration camp. 'We endured terror, beatings, torture and death!' In another group, a Negro boy lowered his collar. 'What about this?' he demanded, showing an ugly rope burn. 'Lynched—for no crime but being black!' In another crowd, there was a pregnant schoolgirl with sullen eyes. 'Why should I suffer?' she murmured. 'It wasn't my fault.'

Far out across the plain there were hundreds of such groups. Each had a complaint against God for the evil and suffering he had permitted in his world. How lucky God was to live in heaven where all was sweetness and light, where there was no weeping or fear, no hunger or hatred. What did God know of all that man had been forced to endure in this world? For God leads a pretty sheltered life, they said.

So each of these groups sent forth their leader, chosen because he had suffered the most. A Jew, a Negro, a person from Hiroshima, a horribly deformed arthritic, a thalidomide child. In the centre of the plain they consulted with each other. At last they were ready to present their case. It was rather clever.

Before God could be qualified to be their judge, he must endure what they had endured. The decision was that God should be sentenced to live upon earth—as a man!

'Let him be born a Jew. Let the legitimacy of his birth be doubted. Give him a work so difficult that even his family will think him out of his mind when he tries to do it. Let him be betrayed by his closest friends. Let him face false charges, be tried by a prejudiced jury, and convicted by a cowardly judge. Let him be tortured. At the last, let him see what it means to be terribly alone. Then let him die. Let him die so that there can be no doubt that he died. Let there be a host of witnesses to verify it.'

As each leader announced his portion of the sentence, loud murmurs of approval went up from the throng of people assembled. And when the last had finished pronouncing sentence, there was a long silence. No one uttered another word. No one moved. For suddenly all knew that God had already served his sentence.

It is quite possible that we can express sorrow or regret through someone else. Sending someone else, however, to apologize for something, to send your condolences, is hardly anything like actually entering into the situation of suffering yourself. The incarnation declares that God suffered in Jesus Christ. God knows, therefore, what it is like to suffer at first-hand; God took human suffering upon himself, lending it meaning and dignity through his presence. To abandon the incarnation is to abandon the idea of a God who enters the world of suffering and sorrows, only to return to a sub-Christian view of God which is an easy target for the criticisms of protest atheism.

In an earlier chapter we noted the impact of the publication in England of John Robinson's book *Honest to God* in 1963. The book was publicized in a newspaper article with the striking headline *Our Image of God Must Go!* It was probably this headline, rather than the somewhat turgid and unoriginal book itself, which caused the greater impact. The image of God which had to go, according to Robinson, was that of an old man in the sky. We have already seen how simplistic and superficial this criticism is. But in the face of the deadly serious criticisms of protest atheism, there is one image of God which *must* go in the modern period—and that is any view of God which sees him as detached from and uninvolved with this world of suffering: in short, a non-incarnational view of God. For traditional Christianity, God suffered in Christ upon the bitter cross of Calvary—he took upon himself the suffering and sin of his creation in order to redeem it. The deadly barbs of protest atheism, which so easily destroy the non-incarnate God of modernism, are impotent against this God—the God who revealed himself to us through Jesus Christ, the *real* God of the Christian faith and not the invented God of modernism. The words of the First World War Christian poet G. A. Studdert-Kennedy evoke this authentic understanding of God with tender insight:

> God, the God I love and worship, reigns in sorrow on the Tree,
> Broken, bleeding, but unconquered, very God of God to me.

The concept of God which results from abandoning the incarnation is simply not a viable option in the twentieth century—it is against precisely this concept of God that the deadly barbs of protest atheism are directed. If this is what God is like, declares this influential movement, we cannot believe in him or take him seriously. Protest atheism has an understandable tendency to select soft targets, and there are few targets softer than a non-incarnational view of God. And the abandonment of such a sub-Christian view of God need not be mourned, for in its place arises the authentically Christian understanding of the God who became incarnate in Jesus Christ. Once more, the crucial importance of the incarnation is evident.

A third point concerns the interpretation of the cross. For some modern theologians, the cross is to be interpreted as nothing more than a demonstration of the love of God. The concept of the incarnation is to be abandoned, we are told, as a logical contradiction. The idea of the death of Jesus Christ upon the cross (and note that these modern theologians do not regard that death as reversed or overturned by the resurrection!) as demonstrating the love of God for us, however, is regarded as acceptable to a 'world come of age'. Unfortunately, it is obvious that this idea is dependent upon that of the incarnation. Let us follow this argument through.

The tender and authentically Christian insight that the death of Jesus Christ upon the cross reveals the full extent of the love of God for us is ultimately grounded in the recognition that it is none other than the Son of God who is dying upon the cross (John 3:16; Galatians 1:4; 2:20; Titus 2:14). Jesus Christ, the incarnate God, loved us and gave himself for us upon the cross of Calvary. While we were still sinners, God stooped down and gave himself up to the nails of the cross—all for the love of sinful humanity (Romans 5:8). The words of William Blake in *Jerusalem* capture this point rather well:

> Jesus said: wouldst thou love one who never died
> For thee, or ever die for one who had not died for thee?
> And if God dieth not for man and giveth not himself
> Eternally for Man, Man could not exist; for Man is love
> As God is love.

But what remains of the cross if we deny that it is God incarnate who died upon its outstretched arms? We are told by these modern theologians that Jesus was no more than a splendid example of humanity—a human being, better in degree than us, but a human being none the less on that account. On the cross, therefore, we see a man losing his life. He did not give his life in the place of anyone else, except possibly Barabbas (Matthew 27:15-26). He was unjustly executed, like all too many before him and all too many after him, as a criminal. It might well be possible to speak of his death as demonstrating, in some rather obscure way, the love of one man for his fellow human beings. But God is not involved. It is not God who is nailed to the cross. It is not something which affects God directly in any way. In short, it is quite improper to speak of the cross showing the love of God for humanity. If anything, it merely illustrates one possible way (and certainly not the only or the best way) in which one human being may demonstrate his love for others. Is this really the foundation of a faith which goes out to conquer the disbelief of the world? It may be easier to believe this than to believe in God incarnate giving himself for us upon the cross—but, in comparison, it is hardly worth believing.

Many critics of the incarnation seem to think that the idea of Jesus being God and man is an arbitrary and irrational dogma invented by some mentally defective thinkers in a period which saw some fairly lousy thinking in the first place. For some modern writers, the demand for belief in the divinity of Jesus is seen as an absurd entry condition for church membership—should not church membership be open to everyone? Why should they be forced to believe in such an irrational and arbitrary edict before they can join a church? No other club or society makes such absurd demands of potential members. The Christian response to this outburst is simply that it rests upon an elementary misunderstanding. Let's illustrate this by looking at a less theological illustration.

Let's suppose you're about to make an omelette. You go into the kitchen, and there you discover three notices, each of which lays down conditions you must observe if you're going to make an omelette. The first declares that you may only make omelettes if you are wearing black leather shoes. The second insists that you must stand with one hand behind your back and recite the Declaration of Independence as you make the omelette. The third demands that you break the eggs before you are allowed to make the omelette. How would we respond to those three? The first two we would dismiss as arbitrary, perhaps invented by the manufacturers of black leather shoes or misguided patriots—they bear no relation to the process of making omelettes. The third, however, is simply a recognition of the realities of omelette-making—you can't make an omelette without breaking eggs. No amount of arguing is going to change that—it will merely delay the production of the omelette.

Critics of the incarnation seem to think that it's in the same class of arbitrary edicts as the first two omelette regulations. But more enlightened thinkers will realize that it's simply a statement of the way things are. Just as the relation of egg shells, egg contents and omelettes demands that the eggs be broken to make an omelette, so the relation of God, humanity and Jesus is such that we are obliged to recognize that Jesus is both God and man. It is an insight into the nature of things, a statement of the nature of reality as Christianity has grasped it. The reasons for making this assertion are excellent, and cannot be dismissed on the basis of such flimsy criticisms. The Christian church affirms that, in the end, everything it stands for rests upon the recognition of the divinity of Jesus—it is not making an arbitrary demand for membership, but stating the crucial and fundamental insight with which it stands or falls.

The Christian gospel proclaims and affirms that God—the living God, the same God who created the universe and us—went to the cross of shame for love of us, sinners though we are. The incarnation gives and guarantees the meaning of the cross as the demonstration of the love of God for us. Deny the former, and the latter is denied along with it. All too often, many modern critics of Christianity seem to assume (for they rarely trouble themselves to prove) that they can eliminate elements of Christian faith which they find objectionable, leaving what remains virtually untouched. They seem to assume that there is some sort of religious equivalent of precision surgery that can cut out one small part of the body without affecting the rest. Now, this is fine with an organ like the appendix which serves no useful purpose, but what about the heart or the brain? Cut these out and the body ceases to function. These organs are essential to the well-being of the body, so closely are they related to other organs, and so many are the organs which depend upon them. It is obvious that the doctrine of the incarnation is like the human heart, rather than the appendix. Eliminate it, and the fabric of the Christian faith unravels; the power-house of the faith ceases to pulsate. When a human heart stops beating, it is merely a matter of time before death occurs. It may be possible to delay that moment through artificial means such as life-support systems, but a state of suspended animation, leading only to death, is the inevitable result.

So it is with any form of Christianity which abandons faith in the incarnation—it is merely a matter of time before it dies. It may retain the outward signs of life for some time, but an irreversible and fatal process of decay has set in. One of the more curious features of criticisms of the doctrine of the incarnation is that they tend to be self-defeating. Those who criticize the incarnation all too often seem to end up with a dull, bookish form of Christianity, lacking any real vitality and excitement, incapable of converting anyone. A theology which is pure and abstract means the end of any living knowledge and a complete detachment from human existence, as the Russian thinker Nicolas Berdyaev so convincingly argued. As a matter of history, it seems that where Christianity is spreading actively and forcefully, it does so on the basis of a firm and convinced faith in the resurrection of Jesus Christ, the incarnate God. To reject that faith—for example, by becoming a Unitarian—is to follow a road which has proved historically to be a spiritual and theological dead-end, leading nowhere.

In this chapter we have been looking at the importance of the incarnation—the recognition that Jesus Christ is none other than God himself. This crucial insight can be justified on both the basis of the New Testament evidence and the Christian experience of God in the risen Christ. It is also essential to the fabric of the Christian faith. Remove or deny this insight, and the Christian faith, like a woollen garment, begins to unravel, lose its shape, and become of no significance. The alternatives offered by those who would have us become 'modern' are not merely unjustified—they are totally inadequate, incapable of coherently conveying Christian insights which even many 'moderns' recognize as essential. They may be of interest to bookish people who like reading Proust and listening to Shostakovich, but they are of no relevance to, they possess no vitality or power for, the vast majority of humanity who know their need for redemption but see in the 'modern' understanding of Jesus no more than a academic moralist incapable of understanding, let alone redeeming, their situation. But for Christianity, God meets people precisely where they are—because he has already been there himself.

The doctrine of the incarnation allows—indeed, it demands —that we recognize that the only really accurate and reliable picture of God which the world has ever been shown is in Jesus Christ. One of our difficulties in thinking about Jesus as God is that we tend to bring our own ready-made ideas of God (wherever we may have found them), to the person of Jesus and then try to make him fit in with our concept of God. But if we take the idea of a revelation of God in Jesus Christ with the seriousness it demands and deserves, we must be willing to have our understanding of God changed, even revolutionized, by what we find. God, as C. S. Lewis so frequently pointed out, is the Great Iconoclast—the one who breaks down our preconceived idea of what he's like so that he can make himself known to us as he really is. And our simple view of God is wrecked by the insight that Jesus is God.

Given that Jesus *is* God, doesn't this say something very important about God himself? Doesn't it mean that God is to be identified with Jesus? How, then, can we avoid suggesting that Jesus is a second God? After all, did not Jesus pray to God? And was not God in heaven during the earthly ministry of Jesus? In asking questions like this, we immediately begin to trace the path which leads to the distinctively Christian understanding of God—the Trinity. We have a long way to go before we arrive there, but by recognizing that Jesus Christ is none other than God incarnate, we have set our feet firmly upon the road that leads to this the most enigmatic of all Christian doctrines. In the following chapter we shall begin to move slowly and carefully down that road as we begin to sketch the outlines of the Christian understanding of the God who revealed himself in Jesus Christ.

7

The Road to the Trinity

To many people, the doctrine of the Trinity is a piece of celestial mathematics—and bad mathematics at that! Why, complained the great rationalist thinkers, should we think of God in so clumsy and complicated a way? Why not just eliminate all this nonsense about 'three-in-ones' and so on, and deal with God instead? After all, the New Testament doesn't talk about God in this way—it talks about God in beautifully simple terms. Thomas Jefferson, third president of the United States, stated this feeling rather well:

> When we shall have done away with the incomprehensible jargon of the Trinitarian arithmetic, that three are one, and one is three; when we shall have knocked down the artificial scaffolding, reared to mask from view the very simple structure of Jesus; when, in short, we shall have unlearned everything which has been taught since his day, and got back to the pure and simple doctrines he inculcated, we shall then be truly and worthily his disciples.

Jefferson's words will strike a chord of sympathy with many a reader, as they once did with this writer. Surely Christianity is a very simple religion: the assertion that God loves us and redeems us through Jesus Christ. But the nagging question

110

underlying the more critical reader of these words is this: is God really so simple that we can understand him, that we can capture him in such simple terms as Jefferson suggests? The wise and challenging words of Augustine are worth remembering: 'If you can understand it, it's not God.'

An illustration will help us think about this. Imagine an iceberg, chillingly white on a cold blue polar sea, majestically drifting towards warmer latitudes, there to melt. Its rugged features are there for all to see, contrasted against the sea. And yet, as we contemplate this iceberg from a passing ship or aeroplane, it is all too easy to overlook something about that iceberg—the simple fact that what we can see is only a fraction of its bulk. Perhaps as much as nine-tenths of it is hidden from our view beneath the water-line. It really is there—it is unquestionably part of that iceberg—but it cannot be seen from above the water-line: all that is presented to our view is its tip.

Perhaps another illustration will help us as we begin to explore the doctrine of the Trinity. Imagine that it is a cold and frosty winter night, and the features of the landscape are picked out by the light of the moon. As you look towards the moon you wonder what it is like. From one night to another you sketch the features you can see, perhaps aiding the naked eye with field glasses or a telescope. And as you sketch, night by night, you begin to realize that part of the moon is permanently hidden from your view—only half of its face can ever be seen from earth. You later discover that this is because of the similarity of the rotational period of the moon about its own axis and about the earth, so that the moon more or less keeps the same face presented to the earth—an unhappy celestial accident which meant that the far side of the moon was a mystery until orbiting satellites photographed its hidden features and relayed them to earth. Even though the far side of the moon could not be seen from earth, it was known to be there—the satellites merely told us what it was like.

A final example is worth noting. Let's suppose you plant a seed in the ground—a bean, say. You then watch the ground carefully for signs of action (like Mr Pooter watched his mustard and cress in *Diary of a Nobody*). Initially nothing seems to happen at all (notice how Jesus draws out the implications of this in Mark 4:26-29). Even though nothing can be seen from the surface of the ground, however, the seed is growing in secret. If we were to dig up the ground at the point where the seed was planted, we would be able to see the root and stalk developing. Eventually, the shoot breaks through the surface of the earth. But there is more to the growing plant than that shoot. Beneath the surface, hidden from view, lies the root system—a central part of the plant which remains unseen from the surface.

In all these examples, we have seen one common factor: the vantage point of the observer stops him from seeing whatever he's looking at in its totality. In other words, the point from which we have to look at something determines how much of it we can see. If you're in a boat on the surface of the sea, you only see the tip of the iceberg—but there's a lot more to that iceberg than what you can see. If you're on the surface of the earth, you can only see half of the surface of the moon—the far side remains hidden from your gaze. And if you're looking at a plant from the surface of the ground, you can only see the bit which is above ground—the root system remains hidden. And for human beings like us, who live on the surface of the world, we can only apprehend a fraction of the reality of God. There is simply far more to God than meets the eye.

Let's develop this point with reference to the iceberg. The bit of the iceberg which we notice, which attracts our attention, is its tip. It is the tip of the iceberg which stands out. Some might be tempted to conclude that this is all there is to the iceberg—the bit that we can see. But, as can be shown without too much difficulty, the vast bulk of the iceberg is there to be discovered. Similarly, what we know about God seems very simple—the great affirmation that God loves us, meets us in Jesus Christ, and takes us home to him. But this is just the tip of the theological iceberg. If we begin to explore what God must be like if he is able to act in this superficially simple way, we discover that what seemed to be very simple on the surface is actually much more complicated. The great declaration that 'God was reconciling the world to himself in Christ' (2 Corinthians 5:19) turns out to be the tip of the iceberg, and the doctrine of the Trinity the bit which is hidden beneath the surface. In other words, 'God was reconciling the world to himself in Christ' is the shoot of the plant whose root is the doctrine of the Trinity. We shall develop this point shortly. Our attention is first claimed by a useful distinction which can be introduced at this stage—the distinction between *kerygma* and *dogma*.

Between *what*? Let's use two English words instead: 'proclamation' and 'doctrine'. *Kerygma* is a Greek word used frequently in the New Testament meaning 'proclamation', the sort of thing that a herald (Greek: *keryx*) would declare. But what is being proclaimed? In the Old Testament, the proclamation is that God has acted in history to redeem his people. An excellent illustration of *kerygma* is the following passage:

> How beautiful on the mountains are the feet of those who bring good news, who proclaim peace, who bring good tidings, who proclaim salvation, who say to Zion, 'Your God reigns!' Listen! Your watchmen lift up their voices; together they shout for joy. When the Lord returns to Zion, they will see it with their own eyes. Burst into songs of joy together, you ruins of Jerusalem, for the Lord has comforted his people, he has redeemed Jerusalem (Isaiah 52:7-9).

The 'proclamation' is the good news of God's redemptive action in history, and so it is hardly surprising to find that the New Testament is full of the proclamation of God's saving activity in the death and resurrection of Jesus Christ (Acts 5:42; 17:23; Romans 10:8; 15:19; 1 Corinthians 11:26; Colossians 1:28; 4:4; 1 John 1:1). According to Acts, the apostles 'never stopped teaching and proclaiming the good news that Jesus is the Christ' (Acts 5:42).

Doctrine is something rather different, however. It is basically concerned with correlating all the aspects of Christian faith and bringing them together into a coherent unity. Doctrine is to proclamation what wine-skins are to wine—something to contain it, to give it shape and strength. It is like a trellis upon which a climbing rose might be grown, or the steel mesh of reinforced concrete—something which creates a framework, a *structure*, which supports something else. Doctrine is about exploring the consequences of Christian faith, making sure that every aspect hangs together properly. To develop this point, we must consider the relation between 'doctrine' and 'proclamation', between *dogma* and *kerygma*.

Let's consider something which you might hear a preacher declare in a sermon, as he unfolds the importance of Christianity for his audience: 'We come to God through Jesus Christ—he is the way back to God for us. If you want to find God, here is where you look—right in the face of Jesus Christ. Here is God, coming up to meet us right where we are, here and now. And through the death and resurrection of Jesus Christ, the way back to God is opened up.' It shouldn't be too difficult to improve on this, but it allows us to make a point. What the preacher is concerned with is *proclamation*: the setting out of the relevance and importance of Jesus for his hearers. Now consider what the theologian would say: 'Jesus Christ is both God and man: he is God incarnate.'

Now, what the theologian is saying seems much less attractive and exciting than what the preacher has to say. But can you see that what the theologian is saying is really something like this: 'Look, preacher, what you are saying depends upon recognizing that Jesus is both God and man—that he is God incarnate. If he isn't God, then he is entirely irrelevant to any thought about God; and if he isn't human, then he is entirely irrelevant to any experience of human life. In other words, the challenging message you were rightly delivering makes certain presuppositions about Jesus which we have to make sure we can justify and defend.' And here we see the basic relation between doctrine and proclamation, between *dogma* and *kerygma*. Doctrine is taking the trouble to think through the implications of the proclamation, and making sure that these implications are understood by those whose business it is to defend Christianity against its critics.

This point is difficult but important. Once it is understood, the way is open to grasping the distinctive role that the doctrine of the Trinity plays in Christian thinking. What we are leading up to is simply this: the *proclamation* is that 'God was reconciling the world to himself in Christ'; the *doctrine* is that the 'God' in question has to be thought of as a Trinity if this proclamation is valid. Or, to go back to our iceberg analogy: the tip of that iceberg is the proclamation—the bit which we first encounter. But on further exploration, we discover the doctrine, the part which is already there, but which we didn't realize was there until we began to explore further.

Let's put this in another way. When you are explaining what Christianity is all about to your interested friends, you needn't mention the word 'Trinity' at all. You speak to them about God, and about the way in which God has revealed himself to us and reconciled us to himself through Jesus Christ. But if you were to sit down and start thinking about the question 'What must God be like if he is able to act in this way?' you will end up with the doctrine of the Trinity. In other words, the doctrine of the Trinity is the end result of a long process of thinking about the way in which God is present and active in his world. It is the result, not the starting-point, of a long process of thinking which can be seen going on in the first four centuries of the Christian era, as Christian theologians wrestled with God's self-revelation in Scripture and tried to understand it. The *proclamation* is that God redeems us in Jesus Christ—the *doctrine* is that God must therefore be a Trinity. It doesn't explain why God is like this, and neither does it pretend to—it simply states that God *must* be like this if he acts in the way in which Christians know that he does.

An illustration may help bring this difficult but important point out. Centuries ago it was noticed that pieces of amber, if rubbed with a dry cloth, suddenly began to attract dust or small pieces of paper. Nobody was quite sure why it behaved in this way, but it unquestionably did behave in this way. As the centuries passed, and studies on this curious phenomenon proceeded, it was realized that this was an instance of the generation of static electricity through a process of ionization. In other words, beginning with the fact that amber did behave in this way, the implications of this observation were unfolded scientifically. The scientific basis of the observation was established. Now it will be obvious that we can make a distinction between two things:

(1) The fact that amber, when rubbed with a dry cloth, attracts bits of paper.

(2) The general principles of static electricity, as these are now understood.

The first is the observation, the second is the theoretical framework within which this observation is set.

Applying this illustration to the doctrine of the Trinity, we can make a distinction between two things:

(1) The fact that 'God was reconciling the world to himself in Christ'.

(2) The doctrine of the Trinity.

The first is the proclamation of the fact that God acts in this specific way; the second is the theoretical framework within which this observation is set, the understanding of the nature of God which follows on from the recognition that he acts in this specific way. This insight also helps us with a slight difficulty which is sometimes emphasized by some modern theologians, anxious to discredit the doctrine of the Trinity. If you look at the doctrine of the early church during the first two and a half centuries or so, you find that the doctrine of the Trinity has yet to be developed. The theologians of the period are well on the way to developing the doctrine, but it hasn't yet appeared in its definitive form. That development took place in the third or fourth centuries. And so, argue critics of the doctrine, this proves that it's not an essential element of Christianity.

Our response to this argument is quite simple. As we have seen, the doctrine of the Trinity is basically an attempt to bring together the incredible richness of the Christian understanding of God. It is the distillation of the kaleidoscopic Christian experience of God in the light of its scriptural foundations. The scriptural witness to and Christian experience of

God came first, and reflection on it came later. In view of the complexity of that experience, it is little wonder that it took so long for the theologians of the church to wrestle with the implications of their faith, and find the best way of describing the God whom they knew in so rich and diverse a fashion. The basic facts (such as the biblical witness to the action of God in history) and the fundamental experiences (such as the experience of an encounter with God through the risen Christ) which *gave rise* to the doctrine had always been known—what was still in a process of development over the first few centuries was the investigation of the *implications* of these facts and experiences.

Let's look at another historical example to bring this point out—a mathematical example, this time. How do you go about working out the area enclosed by a curve, or the volume enclosed by an irregular shape? The classical period saw a number of ingenious geometrical ways of doing this being developed. In the late seventeenth century, however, Newton and Leibniz independently developed the mathematical science of *calculus* which allowed these problems to be analysed directly, without having to go through the complicated classical procedure. The story of this development is known to just about everyone who has ever studied mathematics. But what did Newton and Leibniz actually *do*? Basically, they discovered a new tool for handling numbers. They were able to bring together in a single method what the classical period had treated as a number of problems. What they invented was a sophisticated way of bringing together and developing methods which were already known. Now the older methods were not wrong—they were just shown to be rather clumsy and inelegant compared with the new method.

The parallels with the doctrine of the Trinity will be obvious. The doctrine of the Trinity is a tool which enables the remarkably complex biblical witness to God to be brought together in a more sophisticated whole. It is a way—in fact, really the only way—of making sense of the biblical witness to God. It takes what is already there, what is already known, and shows how it is all related together as a consistent whole.

It is a tool, a method, for handling the kaleidoscope of biblical affirmations about the nature and character of God, and bringing them together. And as it took thousands of years to develop the method of calculus, we can hardly complain that it took the Christian church a mere few centuries to bring together in a single and consistent whole the profundity and richness of the Christian experience of God.

In the following chapter, we shall begin to consider precisely what this Christian experience of God which leads to faith in the Trinity might be.

8

God as Three and God as One

Once upon a time there was a committee. It had three members. Now committees are things which exist to find something to do. And so they set up a project. It was a complicated and long-term development project which took a long time to get off the ground. But it eventually got going, and the committee was pleased with the way it seemed to be working. The project was a long way from the committee's offices, however, so communication was something of a problem. Soon the project developed some teething problems, so the chairman paid occasional visits to it, firing some of its directors and hiring new ones. But things got worse, and the committee realized that it would have to monitor the project on a more long-term basis. So the three of them decided that one of them would have to spend some time living and working on the project, and put things right. But which one would it be? 'Not me!' said the chairman. 'Someone has to stay back at the office and keep an eye on things here.' And so the other two committee members drew straws, and the short straw was drawn by Mr Davidson. So Mr Davidson was sent off to the project. 'Don't forget to keep in touch—and we'll expect a full report from you on your return' were the parting words of the chairman.

This is really a rather pointless story, except that it illustrates only too well the way in which a lot of Christians think about the Trinity! In their thinking, Jesus is basically one member of the divine committee, the one who is sent down to earth to report on things and put things right with the creation. Earlier we looked at biblical models of God (chapter 4), but nowhere in Scripture is God modelled on a committee. The idea of an old man in the sky is bad enough, but the idea of a committee somewhere in the sky is even worse! What, we wonder, might be on their agendas? How often would the chairman have to cast his vote to break a tie between the other two? The whole idea is ludicrous. But how did it develop? Why do some Christians think in this way? The answer is simply that they have been taught about the Trinity so badly that this gross misunderstanding is virtually inevitable. In the remaining chapters we propose to explore *why* it is that Christians believe in the Trinity, and *what* it is that they believe about it.

Where must our discussion start? Perhaps from the most obvious of all places—the conviction of both Old and New Testament writers that there is only one God, and that is the God of Abraham, Isaac and Jacob. 'Hear, O Israel: the Lord our God, the Lord is one' (Deuteronomy 6:4)—a theme taken up, endorsed and echoed by the New Testament writers (Mark 12:29; 1 Corinthians 8:6; Ephesians 4:6; 1 Timothy 2:5; James 2:19). The four points in the Old Testament in which God speaks of himself in the plural (Genesis 1:26; 3:22; 11:7; Isaiah 6:8) are usually understood as 'plurals of majesty', or 'the royal we', although many Christian writers, such as Augustine, argued that these verses already contained hints of a trinitarian way of thinking. At no point in the New Testament is any suggestion made that there is any God other than he who created the world, led Israel to freedom, and gave her the Law at Sinai. The God who liberated his people from their captivity in Egypt is the one and the same God who raised Jesus Christ from the dead.

The New Testament emphasizes that there is only one God (Matthew 23:9; Mark 10:18; 12:29; John 5:44; 17:3; Romans 3:30; 1 Corinthians 8:4, 6; Galatians 3:20; Ephesians 4:6; 1

Timothy 1:17; 2:5; James 2:19; 4:12; Jude 25). It is also clear that God is not *identified* with Jesus: for example, Jesus refers to God as someone other than himself; he prays to God; and finally he commends his spirit to God as he dies. At no point does the New Testament even hint that the word 'God' ceases to refer to the one who is in heaven, and refers solely to Jesus Christ during the period of his earthly existence. This may seem a trivial observation, but it is actually rather important.

Let's pause for a moment and see how far we've got. What we have seen so far is that both Old and New Testaments are united in their assertion that there is only one God, and that 'God' is to be distinguished from Jesus Christ. So far, so good. Earlier we noted Thomas Jefferson's complaints about the 'incomprehensible jargon of the Trinitarian arithmetic', but so far we haven't encountered any difficulties at all.

The difficulties really begin with the recognition of the fundamental Christian insight that Jesus is God incarnate: that in the face of Jesus Christ we see none other than the living God himself. Although the New Testament is not really anything like a textbook of systematic theology, there is nothing stated in the great creeds of the church which is not already explicitly or implicitly stated within its pages. Jesus is understood to act *as God and for God*: whoever sees him, sees God; when he speaks, he speaks with the authority of God; when he makes promises, he makes them on behalf of God; when he judges us, he judges as God; when we worship, we worship the risen Christ as God; and so forth. The New Testament even hints that he was active in the process of creation itself (John 1:3; Colossians 1:16; Hebrews 1:3). Jesus is the one who can be called God and Lord, who acts as creator, saviour and judge, who is worshipped, and to whom prayers are addressed.

It will now be obvious that we are beginning to wrestle with the real problem at issue: in one sense, Jesus is God; in another, he isn't. Thus Jesus is God incarnate—but he still prays to God, without giving the slightest indication that he is talking to himself! Jesus is not *identical* with God in that it is obvious that God continued to be in heaven during Jesus' lifetime, and yet Jesus may be *identified* with God in that the

New Testament has no hesitation in ascribing functions to Jesus which, properly speaking, only God could do. One way of dealing with the problem was to refer to God as 'Father' and Jesus as 'Son' or 'Son of God' (e.g., Romans 1:3; 8:32; Hebrews 4:14; 1 John 4:15), thus indicating that they had the common stock of divinity, but that they could be distinguished, with the Father being thought of as being in some way prior to the Son.

The situation is made still more complex, rather than resolved, through the New Testament's insistence that the Holy Spirit is somehow involved in our experience of both God and Jesus, without being *identical* to either of them (John 16:14; 20:22; Acts 5:9; 8:39; 16:7; Romans 8:9, 26, 34; 1 Corinthians 3:17-18; 1 John 4:2; 5:8). In some sense, Jesus Christ *gives*, or is the *source of*, the Spirit, but the Spirit and Jesus cannot be directly *identified*. The Spirit of God, which the Old Testament recognized as being present in the whole of creation, is now experienced and understood afresh as the Holy Spirit of the God and Father of our Lord Jesus Christ.

Before we continue any further, we must consider the relation between God and Jesus in more detail. The main point that requires careful discussion is this: if Jesus *is God*, does this not imply that God *is Jesus*? In other words, if Jesus Christ is God, must we not draw the conclusion that God is to be identified totally with Jesus Christ? And yet, as we saw above, it is obvious from Jesus' own teaching that he thought that God was still very much in heaven! The paradox we're beginning to wrestle with is expressed well by St Germanus in his famous seventh-century Christmas hymn:

> The Word becomes incarnate
> And yet remains on high!

But does not this call into question the traditional Christian affirmation that Jesus *is* God? Perhaps some illustrations may begin to cast some light on the basic problem we're facing here.

Let's suppose that you are on a liner as it crosses the Atlantic Ocean from Europe to America. The journey makes a deep impression upon you as you watch the great ocean swell bursting against the ship and covering it with salty spray. You can feel the great untamed power of the ocean as it tosses the liner to and fro. You are overwhelmed by its sheer immensity as day after day passes without any sight of land. But have you actually experienced the Atlantic Ocean? Your immediate answer would be an indignant 'Of course I have!' But on reflection, you might begin to realize the difficulty which lies behind this simple question.

Think of how vast the Atlantic Ocean is: its untold depths, its enormous span from North America to Europe, from one icy polar sea to another. Think of the enormous volume of water which goes to make up its bulk. Did you *really* experience and encounter *all* that water? After all, your liner cut a remarkably narrow and shallow path through that ocean. In terms of the sheer bulk of the ocean, you probably experienced an infinitesimally small percentage of that ocean. So your claim to have experienced it would have to be called into question. You may have sampled a tiny fragment, but you didn't experience the whole thing. While accepting this point, you would, however, have every right to insist that you *did* experience the Atlantic Ocean. You know what it is like through encountering it at first-hand. There is just no way that you could have encountered every single molecule of North Atlantic water, but you did have a real first-hand experience of what that ocean is like.

Let's take another example to make this point clear. Like many people, I vividly remember the moment when a human being set foot on the moon for the first time. It was astonishing to think that history was being made before our very eyes as we watched the television pictures being relayed from the moon, showing Neil Armstrong setting foot on alien ground for the first time. And that same Apollo team brought back samples of moon-rock from that mission, so that they could be analysed on earth. Now, through the analysis of that rock we came to know more about the moon. True, it was only a sample of the moon that was brought back to earth (to bring the whole moon back would not have been a particularly realistic possibility), but it allowed us a *direct* encounter with the substance of the moon. It really was the moon which was being studied in laboratories throughout the world after the Apollo mission.

With these illustrations in mind, let's come back to the question of the relation between Jesus and God. The doctrine of the incarnation affirms that it really is God who we encounter in Jesus Christ, but that this does not allow us to assert that Jesus and God are identical. In the illustrations we find the same difficulty being experienced. On the one hand, the moon-rock *isn't* identical with the moon (after all, the moon is still there in the night sky); on the other, it *is* identical with the moon in that it lets us find out what the moon is like—it is a representative sample of what the moon is like.

Let's develop this moon-rock illustration further. Until about 1950 we knew the moon only as a distant object. It was something far away which we could only find out about by looking at it through our telescopes. But when the first samples of moon-rock were brought back, we suddenly knew about the moon in a new and direct way. In a way God is like the moon. Before Jesus Christ came, we knew about him in a rather distant way. And then suddenly, on account of the incarnation of Jesus Christ, we knew him in a new, direct and exciting way. Of course, this new advance didn't come about because of some human technological advance, but through God's decision to become incarnate, to make himself known to us in Jesus Christ. And so where before God could have seemed to be little more than a distant idea, he now becomes a person. And just as people were excited about holding the first moon-rock, and knowing that they held in their hands a bit of the same moon which illuminated the night sky, so the first Christians got excited about being able to touch the one who was none other than God incarnate. (1 John 1:1-4 conveys this excitement well.) We don't need to figure out who God is and what he is like, because he has taken the initiative and told us.

Let's suppose that you are back at high school, and you are asked to find out what gases are present in air. How would you go about doing this? Perhaps the most obvious way would be to take a sample of the air in a small container, and then submit this sample to chemical or physical analysis. And on the basis of the analysis of that small sample, you could say what gases are present in the air. Now, what is the relation of that small sample of air to the earth's atmosphere? Obviously, they aren't identical. All the earth's atmosphere hasn't been compressed into your small container. But on the other hand, that sample *really is air*—it allows you to find out what the air is like. It doesn't exhaust the earth's atmosphere, but it does allow you to find out what it is like.

Jesus allows us to sample God. This is a remarkably helpful way of beginning to think about the incarnation. It really is God whom we encounter, but this doesn't mean that God is *localized* in this one individual, Jesus Christ. Because Jesus *is* God, he allows us to find out what God is like, to have a direct encounter with the reality of God. And because God is not totally identical with Jesus, he remains in heaven, in much the same way as the earth's atmosphere remains there, despite the fact that we've taken a small sample of it. As we have already emphasized in an earlier chapter, God is just too big, too vast, for us to handle—and so God, knowing our weakness and accommodating himself to it (to use Calvin's helpful phrase again), makes himself available for us in a form which we can cope with. The doctrine of the incarnation affirms that it really is God who we encounter directly in Jesus Christ, just as it affirms that God remains God throughout. A similar situation exists in relation to the Holy Spirit. Again, Christianity rightly insists that in the Holy Spirit we really encounter none other than God himself, but that this doesn't mean that God can be said to be *identical* with the Holy Spirit.

How, then, are we to make sense of the complicated New Testament witness to God, Jesus Christ and the Holy Spirit? The situation is clarified if we ask two simple questions. First, when we talk about God, which God do we mean? Secondly, how do we encounter this God? These questions are both of considerable importance in evangelism and preaching, and allow us to begin to gain important insights into the complex biblical witness to Father, Son and Holy Spirit. We begin with the first of these two questions.

Who is the God of Israel? Of course, one answer might be that he is God—there just isn't any other god, and that is all that there is to it. But a more helpful answer to the question would go something like this. The God of Israel is the god who revealed himself to Abraham, Isaac and Jacob; the god who led the people of Israel out of Egypt and into the promised land with great signs and wonders. In other words, we tell a story about God which helps us understand who he is.

We might do the same sort of thing when trying to identify a person. Your conversation with someone might go like this. 'You know John Brown? You don't. Well, do you remember reading about a man who managed to row a boat all the way across the Atlantic Ocean about a year ago? The boat nearly sank at one point. And when he finished the journey, he wrote a book about it. Ah! You *do* know who I mean.' What you are doing here is telling a story which centres on John Brown—you are identifying him in this way. John Brown is the person at the centre of the story—the story is told about him. And so it is with God and the Old Testament. The Old Testament identifies God from the history of his people. The great stories of Abraham, Isaac and Jacob, of the Exodus from Egypt, and so on, are told in order to identify God. The God of Israel is the one who acted in this way.

This is made clear in a number of Old Testament passages (e.g., Exodus 19:4-5; Deuteronomy 26:5-9; Ezekiel 20:5-26). Question: who is God? Answer: whoever got us out of Egypt! Of course, God has a name as well—a name which proves difficult to translate into English, 'Yahweh', 'the Lord' and 'Jehovah' being three of the best-known translations. But the fact remains that God is usually thought of in terms of what he did, rather than in terms of his name.

Now we turn to the God whom Christians worship and adore. Who is this God? To answer this question, the New Testament tells a story—perhaps the most famous story in the world—the story of Jesus Christ. And as that story reaches its climax in the account of the resurrection of Jesus from the dead, we learn that God, for Christians, is the one who acted in this way to raise Jesus. Question: who is the God whom Christians worship and adore? Answer: whoever 'raised Jesus our Lord from the dead' (Romans 4:24). Of course, the New Testament writers make it abundantly clear that the God who 'raised Jesus our Lord from the dead' is the same God who got Israel out of Egypt, but the New Testament emphasis falls upon the resurrection of Jesus.

This idea can be taken further without difficulty. The resurrection of Jesus and the pouring out of the Holy Spirit at Pentecost are treated as closely related by the New Testament writers. The complexity of their statements concerning the relationship of God, Jesus and the Holy Spirit defies neat categorization, but it is clear that 'God' is the one who raised Jesus from the dead, and is now present in his church through the Holy Spirit. In many ways, the Christian formula 'Father, Son and Holy Spirit' (Matthew 28:19; 2 Corinthians 13:14) corresponds to the Old Testament formula 'the God of Abraham, Isaac and Jacob'—it *identifies* the God in question. Question: what God are you talking about? Answer: the God who raised Jesus Christ from the dead, and is now present in the church through the Holy Spirit. The trinitarian formula is a shorthand way of identifying exactly what God we are talking about—it is almost a proper name, in fact. Christianity packs into this one neat phrase the high points of salvation history, the big moments (resurrection and Pentecost) when God was so clearly present and active. It specifically links God with these events, just as Israel specifically linked God with the Exodus from Egypt. It focuses our attention on events in which God's presence and activity were concentrated and publicly demonstrated.

The doctrine of the Trinity is thus a summary of the story of God's dealings with his people. It narrates the story of how God created and redeemed us. It hits the high points of this story, affirming that it is the story of the one and the same God throughout. If you were talking about a great modern statesman, such as Winston Churchill or John F. Kennedy, you would concentrate upon the high points of their careers, the moments when they stepped onto the stage of history in order to change its direction. Similarly, the doctrine of the Trinity identifies those great moments in the history of salvation when God was active *and was seen to be active*. It affirms that God is active in his world, that he is known by what he does, and points to the creation, the death and resurrection of Jesus Christ, and Pentecost as turning-points in his dealings with us. The doctrine of the Trinity thus spells out exactly who the God we are dealing with actually is.

The second question follows on from this: how do we *encounter*, how do we *experience*, this God? Where and how may he be found? The New Testament gives two main answers to this question. First, he may be found in Jesus Christ. Secondly, he may be found through the Holy Spirit. Jesus Christ, as we have seen, is God incarnate: to have seen him is to have seen God; to have encountered him is to have encountered God. But, we might reasonably ask, how do we encounter or experience *Jesus*? The New Testament gives the answer: through the Spirit. The Spirit represents Jesus Christ to us in order that we may gain access to the Father through him.

This idea is developed with great skill in John's gospel. According to John, the Spirit was given after the resurrection with the explicit purpose of glorifying Jesus and revealing the truth about him (John 14:16-17; 16:13-14). Jesus gives the Spirit to his disciples, emphasizing the close personal link between them (John 20:22). The Spirit leads individuals to a knowledge of Jesus and fellowship with him—and through that knowledge of and fellowship with Jesus comes knowledge of and fellowship with the Father. The close link between Father, Son and Spirit is emphasized in a number of ways. Just as the Father sends the Son (John 5:23), so it is he sends the Spirit in the name of the Son (John 14:26). Or, as another passage suggests, it is the Son who sends the Spirit (John 16:7). This is given added weight by the encounter between Jesus and his disciples after the resurrection, in which the Son bestows the Spirit upon them (John 20:22). The Son comes from God (John 16:27) just as the Spirit comes from God, sent by the Son (John 15:26).

We could summarize this complex network of relationships like this:

(1) The Father sends the Son in his name, and the Son is subject to the Father.

(2) The Father sends the Spirit in the name of the Son, and the Spirit is subject to the Father.

(3) The Spirit is sent by the Son, and is subject to the Son.

It will be clear that this set of relationships can be represented in the following manner:

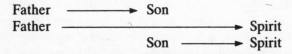

```
Father  ─────────►  Son
Father  ──────────────────────────►  Spirit
            Son  ─────────►  Spirit
```

There is a continuity of relationships between Father, Son and Spirit, thus establishing an unbreakable link between encounter with or experience of the Spirit, the Son and the Father. Incidentally, there is a long-standing (and, it must be said, rather unproductive) disagreement between the Eastern and Western churches over whether the Spirit proceeds from the Father alone, or from the Father and the Son. The intricacies of this debate cannot concern us here.

It is also important to realize that the New Testament tends to think of the Holy Spirit as the Spirit of Christ as much as of God. The Spirit is understood to stand in the closest of possible relationships to Christ, so that his presence among the people of Christ is equivalent to the presence of Christ himself, just as the presence of Christ is treated as being that of God himself. In other words, to encounter the Son is really to encounter the Father and not some demigod or surrogate. To encounter the Spirit is really to encounter the Son and hence the Father. The enormous importance of this is obvious: the believer of today can encounter the living God at first-hand, not through semi-divine or created intermediaries. To affirm the divinity of Father, Son and Spirit is not to suggest that there are *three* gods, but simply that the one God can be encountered in these different ways, all of which are equally valid. It means that God makes himself available, here and now, directly and personally. There is no point in history which stands outside the saving purposes of God.

The doctrine of the Trinity does not *explain* how it is that God is able to be present in this remarkable way—it simply *affirms* that God *is* present and available in this manner. Any understanding of God which makes it inconceivable that he should be personally present here and now is simply inadequate to do justice to the richness of the biblical witness to and Christian experience of God. The doctrine of the Trinity, like the doctrine of the incarnation, is not some arbitrary and outdated dictate handed down by some confused council—it is the inevitable result of wrestling with the richness and complexity of the Christian experience of God.

We can now see why Christians talk about God being a 'three-in-one'. One difficulty remains, however, which must be considered. How can God be three persons and one person at the same time? This brings us to an important point which is often not fully understood. The following is a simplified account of the idea of 'person' which may be helpful, although the reader must appreciate that simplifications are potentially dangerous. The word 'person' has changed its meaning since the third century when it began to be used in connection with the 'threefoldness of God'. When we talk about God as a person, we naturally think of God as being *one* person. But theologians such as Tertullian, writing in the third century, used the word 'person' with a different meaning. The word 'person' originally derives from the Latin word *persona*, meaning an actor's face-mask—and, by extension, the role which he takes in a play.

By stating that there were three persons but only one God, Tertullian was asserting that all three major roles in the great drama of human redemption are played by the one and the same God. The three great roles in this drama are all played by the same actor: God. Each of these roles may reveal God in a somewhat different way, but it is the same God in every case. So when we talk about God as one person, we mean one person *in the modern sense of the word*, and when we talk about God as three persons, we mean three persons *in the ancient sense of the word*. It is God, and God alone, who masterminded and executes the great plan of salvation, culminating in Jesus Christ. It is he who is present and active at every stage of its long history. Confusing these two senses of the word 'person' inevitably leads to the idea that God is actually a committee—which, as we saw earlier, is a thoroughly unhelpful and confusing way of thinking about God. The books suggested for further reading will help clear up this point.

9

God and the Trinity

Most Christians rarely talk about the Trinity—but they talk about God rather a lot. This simple observation is all too often overlooked, for it actually contains an important insight into the purpose and place of the doctrine of the Trinity. For when the Christian talks about 'God', the concept of God he is working with, on being fully unpacked, is found to be trinitarian. In other words, the Christian idea of God is *implicitly* trinitarian, and all that theologians have done is to make *explicit* what is already *implicit*.

Let's look at some examples to bring this out. Christians pray to God almost as a matter of instinct—it seems to come to them naturally. As they kneel down to say their prayers, they are aware that in some way (which is very difficult to express in words) God is actually *prompting* them to pray. It is almost as if God is at work within them, creating a desire to pray, or to turn to him in worship and adoration. Yet God is also the one to whom they are praying! A similar situation arises in worship. Although it is God whom we are praising, we are aware that it is somehow God himself who moves us from within to praise him. Theologians have captured this mystery (but certainly not *explained* it) in the formula 'to the Father, through the Son, and in the Holy Spirit'. In prayer and worship alike, we seem to be brought before the presence of the Father, through the mediation of the Son, in the power of the Holy Spirit.

Now, there is no reason whatsoever why the ordinary believer should want to become a theologian, despite all the protests of those who think that academic theology is a good, splendid and necessary thing. The ordinary believer wants to keep his faith simple, and this wish must be respected. But *underlying* this simple faith is a far from simple concept of God! When the theologian begins to unpack the idea of God which underlies the New Testament witness and Christian experience, a remarkably complex idea, which strains the limits of human reason, begins to emerge. Earlier, we suggested that an iceberg was a helpful illustration of this point: only part of it is seen from the surface, and when you begin rummaging around beneath the surface, you discover there is far more to it than meets the eye. And so it is with God. The God in whom the believer puts his simple faith turns out, on closer inspection, to possess hidden depths.

An illustration may make this point clearer. Suppose you turn on your radio or television. Immediately it starts to receive transmissions, snatching the radio waves from the transmitter and converting them to sound and vision. Now, your simple action was merely that of flicking a switch. But *underlying* this simple action which enables the equipment to receive these signals are things like the theory of electromagnetic radiation and integrated circuit technology, about which most of us know nothing. Yet we don't *need* to know about them in order to use our television receivers. If we were to go into the details of how our television works, so that we can *understand* what happens when we turn it on, we would have to face these complicated things. Now, faith in God is to the doctrine of the Trinity what flicking that switch is to the theory of electromagnetic radiation and integrated circuit technology. We can keep our faith simple, or we can explore its depths—and if we opt for the latter, we'll find that the doctrine of the Trinity is already there, perhaps undetected, in our simple faith in the God who raised Jesus Christ from the dead.

The simple believer may well wish to rest content with affirming that God has redeemed him through Jesus Christ, and that he prays to and worships the God who has redeemed him in this wonderful way. But underlying this deceptively simple confession of faith is a very complicated idea of God. Now, if this *idea* of God is simplified, we don't end up with the simple faith of the believer—we end up with no faith at all! To illustrate this point, let's take a simple view of God—the view which is sometimes referred to as 'classical theism', which thinks of God as the immortal, invisible, omnipotent and omniscient being who brought this world into existence but is not part of it. This sort of idea of God underlies much classical Greek and Roman thinking, and also some modern ways of thinking about God (such as Deism and Unitarianism). It will be obvious that this view of God presents no real intellectual problems—it is easy to grasp, and involves no difficult ideas such as the divinity of Christ or the doctrine of the Trinity. It is exactly the sort of way of thinking about God which so appealed to Thomas Jefferson, as we noted earlier (p. 110).

But what view of God does this imply? It implies a God who is outside space and time, and cannot become involved with it. It implies a God whom we have to discover, rather than a God who makes himself known. It implies a God who is always beyond us, and not a God who comes to meet us where we are. It implies a static, rather than a dynamic, God. It implies a God who created, but cannot redeem. In short, this view of God bears virtually no resemblance to the God who makes himself known to us through Scripture, through the death and resurrection of Jesus Christ, and through Christian experience. And, as a matter of historical fact, it was against precisely this view of God that the early church had to develop its doctrine of the Trinity—in order to prevent the 'God and Father of our Lord Jesus Christ' (1 Peter 1:3) becoming confused with this inadequate and deficient view of God. The Christian church was faced with a choice: it either adopted a God who could be *understood*, but could not *redeem*, or a God who could *redeem*, and yet not be *understood*. Rightly, as events proved, it adopted the second of these two options.

For history has shown that there was no third option available.

The view of God which we loosely termed 'classical theist' is thus easy to understand but totally inadequate to account for the biblical witness to and Christian experience of God. Christians know of God as a dynamic, pulsating activity, something or someone who is alive, and not a static thing 'out there'. Simple faith knows of a God who is active, who makes himself known to us, who comes to us and meets us—and there just isn't any simple way of describing or portraying this God. In other words, once we try to *conceptualize* this simple faith, we discover just how complex and rich the Christian understanding of God really is. We can develop this point by considering a related theological problem.

In the sixteenth century, a very helpful way of thinking about the identity and relevance of Jesus became widespread (although the ideas involved go back to Eusebius of Caesarea). This is often referred to as the 'threefold office of Christ'. Jesus' identity and relevance can be summed up in the trinitarian formula 'prophet, priest and king'. The *prophetic office* concerns Jesus' teaching and his miracles; the *priestly office* concerns his offering made for the sin of humanity upon the cross, and the continued intercession of the risen Christ for his people; the *kingly office* concerns the rule of the risen Christ over his people.

These three categories were seen as a convenient summary of all that Jesus Christ had achieved in order to redeem his people. Jesus is prophet (Matthew 21:11; Luke 7:16), priest (Hebrews 2:17; 3:1) and king (Matthew 21:5; 27:11), bringing together in his one person the three great offices of the Old Testament. Jesus is the prophet who, like Moses, would see God face to face (Deuteronomy 34:10); he is the king who, like David, would establish his reign over the people of God (2 Samuel 7:12-16); he is the priest who will cleanse his people of their sins. Thus the three gifts brought to Jesus by the Magi (Matthew 2:1-12) were seen as reflecting these three functions.

What, then, is being said when Jesus is spoken of as

'prophet, priest and king'? That there are three individuals called Jesus? Certainly not! What is being said is that the one individual, Jesus Christ, assumes the functions of these three great Old Testament offices or institutions. We can put this more precisely by going back to our discussion in chapter 4 where we looked at biblical models of God. When we talk about Jesus being 'prophet, priest and king', we are basically saying that there are *three essential models* which must be used if the full significance of Jesus for us is to be brought out. If only one or two of these is used, a deficient and inadequate understanding of the identity and relevance of Jesus Christ results.

For example, if Jesus is thought of as being a prophet, but not a priest or king, we find his identity and significance reduced to that of a religious teacher. If we think of him as both prophet and king, but not a priest, we find him being portrayed as an authoritative religious teacher who rules over those whom he teaches—but whom he doesn't redeem. Only by bringing all three models together do we build up the authentic Christian understanding of the identity of Jesus: the one who redeems his people, who instructs them and who rules over them with authority.

With this illustration in mind, let us return to talking about God as 'Father, Son and Holy Spirit'. A helpful way of looking at this is to say that *three essential models* must be used if the full depth of the Christian experience and understanding of God is to be expressed adequately. No one picture, image or model of God is good enough—and these three models are essential if the basic outlines of the Christian understanding of God is to be preserved. The first model is that of the transcendent God who lies beyond the world as its source and creator; the second is the human face of God, revealed in the person of Jesus Christ; the third is that of the immanent God who is present and active throughout his creation. The doctrine of the Trinity affirms that these three models combine to define the essential Christian insights into the God who raised Jesus Christ from the dead. None of them, taken on its own, is adequate to capture the richness of the Christian experience of God.

A helpful distinction may be introduced at this point to avoid a misunderstanding (technically, 'Sabellianism'). We need to draw a distinction between God as he actually is, and the way in which God acts and reveals himself in history. In Scripture, we find particular attention being directed to the way in which God acts in history—for example, in creation, redemption and the giving of the Holy Spirit at Pentecost. Now, this might give the casual reader the impression that God is Father at *this* point in time (for example, at creation), and is Son at *that* point in time (for example, on the cross of Calvary). In other words, to put it very crudely, the impression might be given that God is Father until the birth of Jesus, that he is Son until Pentecost, and that thereafter he is the Holy Spirit. In fact, the doctrine of the Trinity affirms that *all* of God's actions reflect the fact that God is eternally what his revelation in history demonstrates him to be—Father, Son and Holy Spirit. It may be that certain actions emphasize that God is Father, just as others may emphasize that he is Son— but God acts as a Trinity throughout all his works. Thus even at creation itself we find reference to the Father, the Word and the Holy Spirit (Genesis 1:1-3).

If God was just 'Father', we would have to think of him as the distant and far-removed creator of this world who never becomes directly involved in its affairs. He would govern it from the safety of heaven, far removed from its problems and dangers, rather like a general directing his front-line troops from the safety of a far-distant, bomb-proof bunker. But Christians know that God just isn't like that. If God was just 'Son', we would have to think of God as being identical with Jesus Christ: Jesus is God, and God is Jesus. All of God is concentrated in Jesus, like a billion quarts in a pint-pot. But Christians know that God just isn't like that. Jesus wasn't talking to himself when he prayed. And the New Testament is most careful to insist upon a distinction between Father and Son, as we have seen: God and Jesus cannot just be identified. If God was just the Holy Spirit, we would have to think of him as just part of the world of nature, caught up in the natural process, or in terms similar to nineteenth-century idealist philosophies. But, once more, Christians know that God just isn't like this. He is not reduced to being part of the natural process, but also stands over and against it.

And so we are forced to recognize the need to bring these three models or ways of visualizing God together, if an authentically Christian view of God is to result. Any one of them is only a starting-point—the other two add perspective and depth. To talk of God as Father is really to talk about a one-dimensional God; to talk about God as Father and Son is really to talk about a two-dimensional God; but to talk about God as Father, Son and Holy Spirit is to talk about a three-dimensional God, God as we encounter him in the real world. Father, Son and Holy Spirit are the essential building-blocks of the Christian understanding of God.

It would certainly be much simpler if God could be totally described using just one of these models instead of all three. Unfortunately, Christians have to deal with God as he is rather than as they would like him to be. Our little intellectual systems find themselves groaning under the strain of trying to accommodate God, like old wine-skins trying to contain new wine. In an earlier part of this book, we saw how difficult it is for human words to capture God. If human words cannot adequately describe the aroma of coffee, to use Wittgenstein's famous analogy, how much less can they describe God! Those who complain about the 'illogicality' of the doctrine of the Trinity seem to work on the assumption that if you can't understand something, it is wrong for that very reason. They cry, 'Contradiction!' and expect everyone to abandon whatever it is that is alleged to be contradictory there and then. But reality just isn't like that.

Much modern science recognizes the fundamental mysteriousness of reality, and that the best we can hope to get is a partial apprehension or grasp of what it's like. Simply because we can only gain a partial glimpse into the way things are, it is inevitable that contradiction of some sort will arise. An example of this from the world of science concerns the nature of light. By the first decade of the twentieth century, it was clear that light behaved in a very strange way—sometimes it seemed to behave as if it was a wave, and sometimes as if it was a particle. It couldn't be both at once, and so the cry 'contradiction!' was raised. How could it be two totally different things? But eventually, through the development of the Quantum Theory, it was found that this contradiction expressed a fundamental difficulty in grasping what the nature of light really was. In other words, the contradiction did not arise on account of light, but on account of our difficulties in conceiving it.

To put this another way, we could return to the idea of a model, discussed in an earlier chapter. The nature of light was such that two contradictory models had to be used to account for its behaviour. No one model was good enough to explain it, and so two—the models of 'wave' and 'particle'—had to be used. The difficulty arose because of the way in which we 'picture' or conceive light, not on account of the nature of light itself. Now, the relevance of this illustration to the doctrine of the Trinity will be obvious. Basically, we are suggesting that God, like light, is very difficult to 'picture'. The difficulty arises simply on account of the way in which we think about God. And where *two* contradictory models of light were needed to account for its behaviour (prior to the development of Quantum Theory), *three* 'contradictory' models of God are required to account for the way in which Christians encounter and experience him.

Let's take this illustration a little further. Most of us know what light is without needing to think about waves, particles or Quantum Theory. Light is what we need in order to see, to do our everyday business, to read and write. It is what comes out of the sun, and to a lesser extent from the moon. It is what we get when we switch on electric light bulbs or strip lighting. If we were physicists, we might want to think about light in much more detail and go into the full complexities of it—and so we might start talking about waves, particles and Quantum Theory. But we don't need to do this in order to make use of light or to recognize it when we see it.

Similarly, most of us know who and what God is without

needing to think about the Trinity. God is the one who created this world and us. He is the 'God and Father of our Lord
Jesus Christ'. He is the one who raised Jesus Christ from the
dead. He is the one who knocks at the door of our life, gently
asking to be admitted. He is the one whom we worship and
adore, and to whom we pray, and so on. Now, if we were
theologians we might like to think about God in more detail,
and that thinking would eventually lead to the doctrine of the
Trinity—and so we would start talking about Father, Son and
Holy Spirit. But we don't *need* to do this in order to encounter
or experience him, any more than we need to be experts on
the nature of light to switch on car headlights. It is not the
doctrine of the Trinity which underlies the Christian faith, but
the living God whom we encounter through Jesus Christ in the
power of the Holy Spirit—the God who *is* the Trinity.

How, then, are we to bring these three models of God
together? Probably because I'm Irish, one of my favourite
people is St Patrick, patron saint of Ireland. Patrick's analogy
for the relation between God and the Trinity was provided by
the shamrock—a three-leaved plant looking rather like
clover, lucerne or alfalfa. Each of the three portions of the
leaf is an essential part of that leaf, but the leaf itself is greater
than its parts. It is the leaf itself which models God, and the
three parts of the leaf which model the individual persons of
the Trinity. A similar analogy is provided by a triangle, with
its three sides, or by a family of two parents and their child.
The individual persons of the Trinity—Father, Son and Holy
Spirit—combine to create a whole in which their individu-
alities are transcended to give a higher unity. Thus when we
think of God, we don't think of three *individual gods*, but of
one God whom we experience and encounter in a three-fold
manner.

The following analogy may help bring out the distinctive
role of the doctrine of the Trinity. Imagine a river—perhaps a
great river, like the Nile or Mississippi—as it enters the sea,
maybe through a great estuary. You wonder what the source
of the river is like and where it might be. Let us suppose that
you own a small boat which you launch into the estuary and

begin the journey upstream to trace the river to its source—
perhaps like the great expeditions of the last century which set
out in search of the source of the Nile. You begin from where
the river rushes in to embrace the sea, and follow the course
of its stream until finally (maybe a very long time later!) you
realize that the great lake which you have just entered has no
other streams entering or leaving it—you have traced the river
to its source.

The first point to make is the following. The estuary, the
stream and the source are all part of the same thing—the
river. All three collectively make up the totality of that river,
and the absence of any of them is unthinkable. A river must
have a source, a flux or stream, and a place at which it enters
the sea or another lake. The eleventh-century theologian
Anselm of Canterbury used the analogy of the River Nile to
make a very similar point.

It is, however, the second point which is more important.
We began the search for the source of that river at the point at
which it met the sea—the point at which its flux, its stream or
flow, entered the sea. It was this point which allowed us to
gain entry to the flux of the stream itself. And it was the
stream itself which both guided us to its source and provided
the means by which we might get there. It pointed the way
and gave us the medium on which the boat could travel safely.
And finally its source was reached—it is here that we found
our journey's end. Can you see that it was the river itself—
from estuary, to stream, to source—which both pointed the
way to and provided the means of reaching our objective? At
every point in the journey, the river itself helped us in our
search, providing both directions and the medium of trans-
port. Although our interest was really in the source of the
river, every point on that river—whether estuary or stream—
derived from that source. We were already encountering the
water from that source as we entered the river estuary. Perhaps it was not immediately recognizable as the water from
that source, but the fact remains that it was the same water.

Let us use this illustration to help us understand the doctrine of the Trinity. The doctrine of the Trinity affirms that,

even as we begin our search for God, it is God who helps us to find him. It is God who sets us on the right path, directs us, and provides us with the means we need to find him. God is involved from the beginning to the end of our search for him, of our encounter with him. It may be that we do not recognize God fully for what he is and what he is doing, but the fact remains that he is involved. God is both the goal of our journey and the means by which we find him. We come to the Father through the Son in the power of the Holy Spirit. At every stage, God is already there. And it is insights such as these that the doctrine of the Trinity is meant to safeguard, by preventing us from adopting inadequate views of God.

In the end, however, it is very difficult to find illustrations for the doctrine of the Trinity—simply because the doctrine is in a class of its own. There is really nothing which can illustrate it adequately, although we can hope to cast light on it in various ways. Earlier we drew attention to the danger of confusing a *representation* of God with the *reality* of God. There is every danger that we will fall into the same trap with the Trinity, by confusing a representation of the doctrine (such as a shamrock leaf or a river) with the Trinity itself, perhaps rejecting the Trinity because we aren't convinced by the illustrations used to represent it. Perhaps it is necessary once more to emphasize the mysteriousness of God—not to discourage thinking about him, but simply to draw attention to the fact that we are never going to be able to describe him adequately.

In this book we have been exploring the Christian understanding of God: the way in which we speak and think about him, the idea of a 'personal God', and finally the doctrine of the Trinity. There is undoubtedly much more that could be said about these, and it could unquestionably be said much better as well. However, it is time to draw the great themes of this book together, as we prepare to conclude.

10

The Strong Name of the Trinity

What sort of animal, my wife and I wondered, should we buy for our son as a pet? Eventually, our thoughts turned to rabbits, and we bought a little book on the subject of . . . rabbits. It was most helpful, describing breeds of rabbits which we had never heard of before, including Flemish Giants. As I read about these enormous rabbits, some words seemed to stand out from the page: 'Caution: these rabbits are too big to be handled by children.' And the book went on to recommend dwarf rabbits—which can be held in the palm of the hand—as ideal children's pets. Isn't this just the way we try to treat God? We try to make him into something which we can handle, something which we can control when in fact God is just too big and too great to be handled by human beings. As Martin Luther once remarked, 'It is God who handles us, and not we who handle God!' We tend to treat God as if he were some kind of pet, something which we can tame, something which we can domesticate.

In the end, the doctrine of the Trinity represents our admission that we cannot tame God to fit our tidy little systems. God just will not fit into the palm of our hands so that we can hold him down! Like the wild West wind in Shelley's *Ode*, he is uncontrollable. Far too many thinkers regard God as some

143

sort of biological specimen, something which can be pinned down beneath a microscope slide to be studied at our convenience and under conditions of our own choosing. Perhaps the famous opening words of Hannah Glasse's eighteenth-century recipe for Hare Soup may show up the basic problem here: 'First catch your hare!'

As we have been arguing throughout this book, the Christian theologian isn't in the position of a geologist studying rocks or a paleontologist studying fossils—all they have to do is go out and find their rocks or fossils. Perhaps it is more helpful to think of the theologian as being like a student of rare butterflies—he has to find *and capture* his specimens. Unlike rocks and fossils, butterflies are very much alive, and are not enthusiastic about being captured! The theologian is forced to admit that the initiative lies with God. We may see hints and hear rumours of God's existence and nature from the world around about us, but the full self-disclosure of God is something which happens on his terms. In other words, God lets us see him in a particular way, and we must take him as and where we find him. God, as we have said before, is not a concept or idea which we can kick around at leisure in our seminar rooms—he is the living God who created the world and us, and who obstinately refuses to surrender himself to our theological dissecting tables.

The doctrine of the Trinity is the response of the Christian community down the centuries as it has responded to and reflected upon God's revelation of himself. Everyone likes simple religions, and there is always a temptation to make Christianity as easy as it possibly can be. But there's a limit to how much you can simplify something which is already very complicated. Try to imagine something very complicated which you're familiar with, and work out how you would explain it in very easy terms to someone else. You will almost certainly find yourself oversimplifying it—as you explain your subject, you will probably find yourself thinking, 'It's not really like this at all, but unless I explain it like this, you'll never understand it.' It is so much easier to think of God in very simple terms—perhaps as the great heavenly ruler of the universe, far removed from this world. But the problem with this is obvious: this isn't just an oversimplification of the Christian understanding of God, it's a serious distortion of this understanding. The really simple religions are actually ones which have been *invented* by human beings.

Christians, then, respond to God as he has revealed himself in Scripture, in Christian experience, and in the life, death and resurrection of Jesus Christ. If Christians had just invented their idea of God, of course, they could simplify it enormously—but the point is that they haven't. They don't have control over God and the way in which he has revealed himself. This is something which is 'given', something which is already there even before we begin to think about it. In the eleventh century, Anselm of Canterbury came up with a formula which is very helpful in understanding this point— 'faith seeking understanding (*fides quaerens intellectum*)'. In other words, faith comes first—and *then* we have to try and understand it.

Imagine an iceberg suddenly floating towards you. In some senses, encountering God's revelation of himself is rather like encountering an iceberg—it's already there, and once we encounter it, we can explore it and find out what it's like. But we can't lay down what that iceberg ought to be like—we have to take it as it comes. Nor is it something we've invented—it is something already there, independent of us. An image of God which we invent is nothing more and nothing less than an idol, and that is why it is so important for the New Testament writers that Jesus Christ is the God-given image of God (see Colossians 1:15). In other words, we are *authorized* by God to use this image of himself. It is an image which has been given to us by God, rather than one which we have invented or made up.

When thinking about God, we can do one of two things. We can invent an idea of God, laying down what God ought to be like in the light of what everyone has said about God during human history, or we can respond to God as he has revealed himself. The difficulty with the former option is that it isn't a realistic option at all. If you look at the ideas of God which human beings have had in history, they have virtually nothing in common. Western philosophy has been obsessed with the idea of God which is sometimes called 'classical theism'—but this bears little relation to the idea of God associated with Hinduism, Buddhism or African tribal religions.

All too often, Western philosophers seem to work on the assumption that they know exactly what God is like, through thinking intelligent thoughts about the universe and reading Platonic dialogues, and that they are thus in a position to pass judgement on what everyone else (such as Christians) says about him. It is as if they have access to some sort of infallible source of knowledge about God which allows them to lay down what God is really like and criticize anyone whose views happen to differ from theirs as being 'philosophically naïve'. The truth of the matter, however, is that God has always proved to be something of an enigma to human reason. All human statements about God, whether made by the Christian believer or a professional philosopher, are matters of faith. That is one of the reasons why the self-revelation of God is such good news.

Against the tendency of human beings to invent or construct their own idea of God and then worship it (which is idolatry) or declare that it's not worth worshipping (which is rationalism), we may set the exciting and deeply disturbing Christian insight that God has taken the initiative in revealing himself to us. Who God is and what he is like—these are matters on which God himself has decided to have the final word. Christian thinkers thus attempt to wrestle with God as he has revealed himself in Scripture, particularly in its testimony to Jesus Christ. And they have every right to resist the criticism of those who suggest that they are being 'philosophically naïve' in doing so. After all, philosophers—who have some difficulty in even reaching any agreement on whether God exists—do not have access to some private and infallible knowledge of God which is denied to everyone else.

For some modern critics of the doctrine of the Trinity, it is obvious that it rests upon a series of the most appalling mistakes, including (to name only the more obvious) mathematical confusion and philosophical unsophistication. Some of these critics seem to think that some early Christian committee had sat down to shape their understanding of God, and—being unable to agree upon how many bits of God there were—thought of a number between one and ten and agreed upon three as a judicious compromise. Like the White Queen in Lewis Carroll's *Alice Through the Looking Glass*, who made a habit of believing six impossible things each day before breakfast, they took a certain pleasure in the absurdity of their ideas. The idea of the God of Christianity being just one, according to some of these critics, was found to be rather demeaning to God, and so it was thought necessary to expand God somewhat to emphasize his greatness and superiority over other gods. Now the early Christians were, of course, very primitive people and, as the latest scholarship had just discovered, primitive peoples could count no higher than three. In other words, they understood 'three' as we would understand 'infinity', so that the statement that 'God is three' really meant 'God is infinite'. And so the idea of God being three, instead of just one (or in addition to being one), came into being as an expression of the infinite superiority of the Christian God over all other gods.

Scholarship has, however, moved on since the 1890s! Primitive peoples, it was discovered, could cope with numbers far in excess of three. And anyway, it was perfectly obvious that the doctrine of the Trinity had nothing to do with mathematics, but was an attempt to express the fullness and richness of the Christian experience and understanding of God. It attempts to capture the mystery of God in a form of words, to distil a host of insights into a formula. It is 'bones to philosophy, but milk to faith' (John Donne). The doctrine of the Trinity is to the Christian experience of God what grammar is to poetry—it establishes a structure, a framework, which allows us to make sense of something which far surpasses it. It is the skeleton supporting the flesh of Christian experience. The Christian experience of God was already there, long before the doctrine of the Trinity was formulated, but the doctrine casts light on that experience and helps us understand *who* it is that we are experiencing. It *interprets* our experience of God *as experience of God*. It eliminates inadequate and unsatisfactory ideas of God which stand in his way—just as we might dredge a channel to allow the current to flow more freely, so the doctrine of the Trinity dredges the channels of our minds, removing obstacles (such as sub-Christian ideas of God) which stand in the path of God as he moves to encounter us.

The doctrine of the Trinity, then, is the Christian's last word about God. It is not something which we begin with, but something we end up with. When you're trying to explain Christianity to someone, the last thing you'd want to talk about is the Trinity. Instead, you might begin by talking about Jesus Christ, about his death on the cross and resurrection, or you might talk about the possibility of encountering or experiencing God here and now. But even as you begin to talk about God in such ways, you are working within the framework established by the doctrine of the Trinity. You could say that the doctrine of the Trinity is latent within the way you're talking about God, and all that theologians have really done is to draw out something which is already there. The doctrine of the Trinity wasn't *invented*—it was *uncovered*. It is something implicit within all Christian thinking about God, and all that theologians have done is to make it explicit. It's like someone drawing a map which shows all the features of the country, thus allowing you to establish how they relate to each other. Those relations are already there—the map just helps make them clearer.

What, then, is the importance of the doctrine of the Trinity? Someone once asked Louis Armstrong what jazz was. 'If you gotta ask what it is, you'll never know!' he replied. And people often ask who or what God is, and expect a slightly more helpful answer. The doctrine of the Trinity is a summary of the Christian's answer to who God is and what he is like. It is like the synopsis of a story—the story of our redemption through the death and resurrection of Jesus Christ. It hits the high points of that story, talking about our creation, our redemption and our renewal. But it is the story of the one and the same God who stoops down to meet his creatures where they are in order to bring them back to him. It is a summary of God's relevance for us, of what God does for us. It is a declaration that the same God who so wonderfully created us has acted even more wonderfully to redeem us.

One of the most powerful of all the Christian church's many hymns is the ancient Irish hymn usually ascribed to Patrick, the patron saint of Ireland, and generally known as 'St Patrick's Breastplate'. In this hymn, the believer is constantly reminded of the richness and the depth of the Christian understanding of God, and that it is this God who has been bonded to the believer through faith:

> I bind unto myself today
> The strong name of the Trinity,
> By invocation of the same,
> The Three in One and One in Three.

It is the power and presence of *this* God which allows the Christian to hold his head up high in a world of darkness and sin.

The hymn then moves on to survey the vast panorama of the works of God in history. The believer is reminded that the God whom he has dared to make his own through faith is the same God who brought the earth into being, and as the believer contemplates the wonders of nature, he may grasp the astonishing insight that the God whose presence and power undergirds the world of nature is the same God whose presence and power is channelled into his individual existence:

> I bind unto myself today
> The virtues of the star-lit heaven,
> The glorious sun's life-giving ray,
> The whiteness of the moon at even,
> The flashing of the lightning free,
> The whirling wind's tempestuous shocks,
> The stable earth, the deep salt sea,
> Around the old eternal rocks.

Our attention then turns to the work of God in redemption.

The same God who created the world—the earth, the sea, the sun, moon, and stars—acted in Jesus Christ to redeem us. In the history of Jesus Christ, from his incarnation to his second coming, we may see God acting to redeem us, an action which we appropriate and make our own through faith:

> I bind this day to me for ever,
> By power of faith, Christ's incarnation;
> His baptism in the Jordan river;
> His death on cross for my salvation.
> His bursting from the spicèd tomb;
> His riding up the heavenly way;
> His coming at the day of doom:
> I bind unto myself today.

The believer is invited to reflect upon the history of Jesus Christ: his incarnation, baptism, death, resurrection, ascension and final coming on the last day. And all these, Patrick affirms, are the actions of the same God who created us, as he moves to redeem us through Jesus Christ. All these were done for us, for the sinful creatures upon whom a gracious God took pity.

Finally, the God who called the universe into being and redeemed us through the great sequence of events which is the history of Jesus Christ is also the God who is with us here and now, who meets us and stays with us:

> I bind unto myself today,
> The power of God to hold and lead,
> His eye to watch, his might to stay,
> His ear to hearken to my need;
> The wisdom of my God to teach,
> His hand to guide, His shield to ward,
> The word of God to give me speech,
> His heavenly host to be my guard.

This is the God who is witnessed to in Scripture and encountered in human experience—the God who broke the mould of human thinking, forcing us to stretch our ideas and categories to their limits in order even to begin to accommodate him. This is no God who wound the world up, like a clockwork mechanism, and then left it to run on its own; this is no God who hurls down dictates from the safety of the Olympian heights; this is no God who is dissolved into, and indistinguishable from, the natural process; this is the God who makes himself known to us and available for us through the death and resurrection of Jesus Christ, 'the God and Father of our Lord Jesus Christ'.

In this book we have been laying the foundations for the Christian understanding of the Trinity. We have been discovering the doctrine of the Trinity as we have reflected on the way in which Christians think and speak about the God who meets us and gives himself to us in Jesus Christ. The reader who wishes to develop his thinking on this doctrine further should consult the books recommended for further reading at the end of this book. The foundations which we have been laying in this book may be built upon, and there is much more that could be said about the doctrine than has proved possible in these pages. It is, however, hoped that the reader will have been stimulated to think about this difficult doctrine of the Christian faith with more confidence than might otherwise have been the case.

The doctrine of the Trinity, then, sums up the astonishingly rich and hard-won insights of Christian believers down the ages into the nature of God. For the theologian, it is a safeguard against inadequate understandings of God; for the Christian believer, it is a reminder of the majesty and mystery of the God who gave himself for his people upon the cross. It does not really help us to understand God, but it does enable us to avoid inadequate ways of thinking about him. Faced with the choice between an invented God who could be understood without the slightest difficulty, and the real God who couldn't, the church unhesitatingly chose the latter option. The believer will still find it easier to talk about 'God' than to talk about 'the Trinity', and need hardly be criticized for doing so. But when that believer begins to reflect upon who this God whom he worships and adores really is, his thoughts will move towards the 'strong name of the Trinity'. It is here that the long process of thinking about God comes to a stop, as we realize that we can take it no further. And it is here that thought gives way to worship and adoration.

> Holy, holy, holy, Lord God Almighty!
> All Thy works shall praise Thy name
> In earth, and sky, and sea;
> Holy, holy, holy, merciful and mighty,
> God in three Persons, blessèd Trinity!

> (Bishop Reginald Heber)

For Further Reading

For an introduction to the insights concerning the identity of Jesus Christ which underlie the doctrine of the Trinity, see Alister McGrath, *Understanding Jesus* (Eastbourne, Kingsway Publications, 1987).

The remaining books suggested for further reading are generally of a more academic nature, but they will allow the interested reader to develop further the arguments found in the present book.

For a discussion of proofs and alleged disproofs of the existence of God, see:

Hans Küng, *Does God Exist?* (London, Collins, 1980).

Richard Swinburne, *The Existence of God* (Oxford, Clarendon Press, 1979).

For further discussion of 'models', see the following:

Ian T. Ramsey, *Models and Mystery* (Oxford, Oxford University Press, 1964).

Ed. F. W. Dillistone 'Talking about God: Models, Ancient and Modern', *Myth and Symbol* (London, SPCK, 1966), pp. 76-97.

For excellent discussions of aspects of the doctrine of God, see:

J. I. Packer, *Knowing God* (London, Hodder and Stoughton, 1973).

Ronald H. Nash, *The Concept of God: An Exploration of Contemporary Difficulties with the Attributes of God* (Grand Rapids, Mich., Zondervan, 1983).

For further discussion of the doctrine of the Trinity, see:

E. Calvin Beisner, *God in Three Persons* (Wheaton, Ill., Tyndale Press, 1984). This short work gives an excellent account of the biblical foundations of the doctrine.

Eds. Carl E. Braaten and Robert W. Jenson, *Christian Dogmatics* (Philadelphia, Penn., Fortress Press, 1984), vol. 1, pp. 83-191. This important essay explores the place of the doctrine in systematic theology.

Royce Gordon Gruenler, *The Trinity in the Gospel of John* (Grand Rapids, Mich., Baker Book House, 1986). A careful study of the Trinity as it is presented in John's gospel. Dr Gruenler has promised to supplement this work with two further books on the Trinity, to which we may look forward.

Alasdair Heron, *The Holy Spirit* (London, Marshall, Morgan and Scott, 1983). This useful book includes a particularly helpful discussion of the differences between the Eastern and Western churches on the role of the Holy Spirit within the Trinity.

Two influential twentieth-century discussions of the doctrine are:

Karl Barth, *Church Dogmatics* I/1 (Edinburgh, Clarke, 1936).
Jürgen Moltmann, *The Trinity and the Kingdom of God: The Doctrine of God* (London, SCM, 1981).

Among God's Giants

by J. I. Packer

'The Puritans exemplified maturity; we don't. We are
spiritual dwarfs… The Puritans, by contrast, were
spiritual giants.'

For all those concerned to be mature Christians, Dr
Packer reveals the amazing depth and breadth of
Puritan spirituality. Awakening us to our own
condition, he presents the Puritans as the positive force
they were in real life, by contrast with the dour
reputation they have unfairly earned. His portrait of
Puritan thought and teaching calls us to renewal in a
time of failing vision and moral permissiveness.

'Likely to become a contemporary classic! Thought through
and scholarly – an excellent book.'
                                                    – Clive Calver

'J. I. Packer provides a model of passionate, holy living for
today's often complacent church. Packer's characteristically
lucid style and penetrating insights into Christians of old
send a vibrant challenge to those of us who follow Christ in
this last decade of the twentieth century. I heartily
recommend this book.'
                                                    – Charles Colson

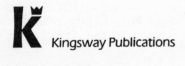

Kingsway Publications

The Applied New Testament Commentary

by Dr Tom Hale
with articles contributed by Dr Stephen Thorson

The *Applied New Testament Commentary* is an easy-to-read, down-to-earth commentary on the text of the New Testament. It can be used with any version of the Bible and includes:

- General Articles on important aspects of the Christian faith
- An introduction to each book of the New Testament

- Word definitions
- Clear explanations of Bible text
- How to apply the Bible to everyday life

'There is very much here for all Bible students to learn, whatever their cultural or denominational background. In fact the *Applied New Testament Commentary* should help to promote mutual understanding, tolerance and respect among Christian people.'

– John Stott

Kingsway Publications

The Cross
God's Way of Salvation

by D. Martyn Lloyd-Jones

When you see the cross of Christ, what do you see?

A man crucified, suffering unjustly in shame and defeat?

No, says Dr Lloyd-Jones: to see the cross as a failure misses the purpose and glory of that momentous event on Calvary's hill. For in Jesus Christ, and particularly in his death, God was carrying out a promise made at the dawn of human history. He was making it possible for imperfect men and women to have a personal relationship with their perfect Creator.

In this book, Dr Lloyd-Jones shows clearly and in depth how this staggering claim is true, and details the far-reaching implications this has for every human being alive today.

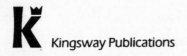 Kingsway Publications

Life in the Spirit

by D. Martyn Lloyd-Jones

In this masterly exposition of the high-priestly prayer in John chapter 17, Dr Martyn Lloyd-Jones demonstrates what Christ has accomplished for us, how he died to sanctify us, and how he desires to be glorified in us.

Here we see the details of God's master plan of salvation hammered out in real-life terms. For while our identity is rooted in God's eternal plan, our experience of God's grace can be a day-to-day reality for every believer.

As you follow the author's inspiring logic, let your mind be enlightened and your heart set ablaze by the depth and majesty of the wisdom of God.

 Kingsway Publications